BROADWAY PLAY PUBLISHING INC

I0170739

CROESUS AND THE WITCH

Adapted from a Century-old
Black Fable by
Vinnette Carroll

Music and Lyrics by
Micki Grant

HANSEL AND GRETEL
(IN THE 1980s)

by
Marie Thomas

Music and Lyrics by
Micki Grant

BROADWAY PLAY PUBLISHING INC
New York
www.broadwayplaypublishing.com
info@broadwayplaypublishing.com

First printing: November 1984

ISBN: 0-88145-024-3

Cover Art by Dixon Scott
Design by Marie Donovan
Set in Trump Mediaeval by Ampersand Publisher Services, Inc.,
   Rutland, VT

Contents

CROESUS AND THE WITCH

Cast

(in order of appearance)

NARRATOR

CROESUS

CHORUS

MATHEW

EPHRAM

HECUBA

Assorted Dancers

(The entire cast and the NARRATOR *enter, talking among themselves. They sit at various places around the stage.* CROESUS *sits upstage, center, on the top step. The* NARRATOR *addresses the audience.)*

NARRATOR: Hello everyone. Welcome to _____. Tonight we'd like to tell you the story of *Croesus and the Witch.* *(She moves toward the musicians and addresses the drummer.)* *(Name of drummer.)* *(She addresses the pianist.)* *(Name of pianist.)* *(At the piano, she starts to sing* STORY TELLING TIME*)*

NARRATOR: Story telling time is here

CHORUS: Story telling time

NARRATOR: Story telling time is here

CHORUS: Story telling time

NARRATOR: Wanna take you someplace that
    you've
Never been,
We'll take you to another time
    and
Bring you back again.

NARRATOR: Story telling time is here

CHORUS: Story telling time

NARRATOR: Story telling time is here

(She starts moving slowly upstage to sit on step at center stage, between legs of Croesus.)

CHORUS: Story telling time,

NARRATOR: Use your imagination, it will be
A treat,
But first I have some friends that I
Would
*(She reaches upstage center and
sits on second step.)*
Like for you to meet:

NARRATOR (con't.)

(The dancers introduce
themselves:)
I am _____.
I am _____.
I am _____.
I am _____.
I am _____.
I am _____.

NARRATOR: And they play—what do you play?

FIRST: Water

SECOND: Deer

THIRD: Acorns

FOUR: Forests

FIFTH: Corn

SIXTH: Mountains, and many, many, . . .

ALL: Many, many, many, many . . . (and on)

NARRATOR: All right!

ALL: Others.

(The cast members introduce themselves.)

MATHEW: I am _____ and I play Mathew.

EPHRAM: I am _____ and I play Ephram.

CROESUS: I am _____ and I play Croesus.

NARRATOR: And I'm _____ and I play guess who? (Cast laughs.)

ALL:

Story telling time is here
Story telling time
Story telling time is here
Story telling time

Wanna take you someplace that
    you've never been
We'll take you to another time,
    and bring
You back again.

>Story telling time is here,
>Story telling time
>Story telling time is here
>Story telling time
>Story telling time is here.

(*During the last few lines, with the exception of the* NARRATOR, *the entire company leisurely exit stage right, stage left, and upstage center.*)

NARRATOR: Once upon a time there was a man named Croesus. Croesus lived a long time ago—in King Solomon's time. You hear folks say, "Mr. Jones is as rich as Croesus." But Croesus wasn't always rich. In fact, Croesus used to be poor—poor as a church mouse—no—even poorer than that—he was as poor as Job's turkey; and you know you can't be poorer than that! I suppose you're wondering how he got so rich, aren't you? Well, in those days deerskin was very expensive—like mink and sable are today.
(*Music; establish forest with projection or other lighting effects. Enter dancers, who become trees in the forest.*) Now, there was this forest . . . (*She moves in and around the trees, and just as they all become deer, she says,*) . . . where lots and lots of deer lived. (*Dancers are spread out over the stage.*) . . . (And in that same forest lived a mean old witch! (*The* NARRATOR *assumes her witch role and runs off stage left.*)

(*Dance number: Deer and Forest. The dancers end up far stage right.*)

NARRATOR: (*Reenters*) Mighty few folks who ventured into that forest ever came out again. Now, like I was saying: this man Croesus (*He enters from stage left.*) was as poor as Job's turkey, but one day he said to himself,

CROESUS: YOU CAN DO WHAT YOU WANNA DO

(*He sings the first line to* NARRATOR *and then shares his philosophy with the audience.*)

>No use sitting, waiting for
>   something
>To happen
>Sitting twiddling your fingers
>   and your
>Toes
>You can be out making your
>   own thing

CROESUS (con't.)

> Happen
> Instead of sitting at home
>   scratching
> Your nose.
>
> You can get what you wanna get
> You can go where you wanna go
> You can do what you wanna do
> By doing it.
>
> Today will be yesterday
>   tomorrow
> If you want to sit around and
>   wait
> You will just be hungrier
>   tomorrow
> And you won't have any grits to
>   put on
> Your plate
>
> You can go where you wanna go
> You can do what you wanna do
> By doing it
> By doing it

(CROESUS crosses to NARRATOR.)

> You can get what you wanna get
> You can go where you wanna go

CROESUS:

> You can do what you wanna do
> By doing it
> By doing it
> By doing it

NARRATOR: Pretty soon the people in the village began to listen, and Croesus called some of his friends.

CROESUS: (Crossing to upstage, center.) Mathew!

MATHEW: (Entering from upstage, right.) Ephram!

MATHEW and EPHRAM: (EPHRAM entering behind MATHEW.) Croesus? (They confer during narration.)

NARRATOR: And they said good-bye to their wives and children, and picked up their bows and arrows, and followed him.

MATHEW:

> OUT THERE IN THE FOREST
>
> Our pockets are empty
> Our cupboards are bare
> The winter is coming

And we've got no winter clothes
to wear

All of our neighbors are as poor
as
Church mice, too
So here's what we'll do

We'll go hunting and kill some
deer
Only as much and no more than
we need.

Everyone will have a deerskin
jacket to wear
Everyone will have sweet
deermeat to eat.
Out there in the forest there are
plenty
Of deer roaming around
Out there in the forest we can
get what we
Need
To feed the people.

ALL THREE: Everyone will have a deerskin
jacket
To wear
Everyone will have sweet
deermeat to eat
Out there in the forest there are
plenty
Of deer roaming around
Out there in the forest we can
get what
We need
To feed the people

Get what we need to feed the
people
Get what we need to feed the
people
Get what we need to feed the
people

NARRATOR: And off they went into the forest to hunt for deer.

(*At the end of the song, the dancers move around the stage to become the forest. The three men move in and about the forest, as some of the trees become deer and then trees again. As the hunters move through the trees the second time, the trees spin around the men and all end up stage right as the men exit upstage, center.*)

DANCE: (*Of the deer running through the forest. They end up at upstage, center, as trees.*)

(*The men enter upstage, right, ready for the kill. The trees become deer and one by one are killed as they run about the stage. Each of the men sings:*)

CROESUS: Got what we need to feed the
                people

MATHEW: Got what we need to feed the
                people

EPHRAM: Got what we need . . .

ALL THREE: . . . To feed the people

(*While singing, the men symbolically skin them as the dancers roll off the stage.*)

THREE MEN: Everyone will have a deerskin
                    jacket to wear
                Everyone will have sweet
                    deermeat to eat
                Out here in the forest there
                    were plenty of
                Deer roaming around
                Out here in the forest we got all
                    that we need
                To feed the people
                Got what we need to feed the
                    people
                Got what we need to feed the
                    people

(*The men pick up the skins and their bows, cross upstage center and exit upstage, lower center. As they reach the upper platform, the NARRATOR enters, passes through them, and ends on the stage left platform.*)

NARRATOR: After a while, night fell, and they sought shelter for the night. Ephram found a path and started (*EPHRAM moves onto stage right platform*) to follow it. (*EPHRAM turns back upstage, goes upstage, center, and calls.*)

EPHRAM: Mathew! Croesus! (*They enter and all cross downstage right onto platform.*)

NARRATOR: It led to a house with light in it, and in that house lived . . .

ALL: Hecuba!

HECUBA: HORRIBLE HECUBA

Hecuba is a mean old witch
With a heart of stone and a bag
      of tricks
To trick ya.
She'll pretend to be nice as pie
But if you look in her evil eye
She'll fix ya.

So hunters, take care
Beware
Of heartless, hateful, horrible
      Hecuba

She lives down in a deep dark
      ditch
With the stolen goods that have
      made her rich
And greedy
She robs the wealthy and
      furthermore
She will even rob the poor
And needy.

So hunters, take care
Beware
Of heartless (MATHEW stands
      straight.),
Hateful (CROESUS and EPHRAM
      straighten.),
Horrible (EPHRAM turns to look
      stage left.)
Hecuba (They all look stage left.).

THREE MEN: We'd better take care
And beware
Of heartless (CROESUS crosses
      left.), Hateful (MATHEW),
      Horrible (EPHRAM crosses.)
      Hecuba
We'd better take care
And beware
Of heartless, hateful, horrible
      Hecuba.

(While singing their third line, the men step down to the ramp; then
they cross left to the stage left platform.)

CROESUS: (*Knocks,* HECUBA *opens the door, and casts spell with her hand before taking* CROESUS' *hand. He says:*) Good evening Ma'am. Can you give us shelter for the night?

HECUBA: (*As an old woman.*) I'm sorry, I don't have any room in my house for you (*They turn away and start stage right.*), but I'll give you the keys to the tool shed. (*They return.*) It's got a fireplace and some chairs to sit on.

CROESUS: Thank you. (*They cross a few steps right.*)

HECUBA: Have you heard tell of Hecuba? (*They stop short.*)

MATHEW: Oh, yes, Ma'am. She that mean . . .

CROESUS: (*Stopping* MATHEW.) Hecuba. No, Ma'am.

HECUBA: She's a mean old witch who roams the forest robbing and killing folks. Beware of her.

(*Men leave the house and head for the stage right platform, the tool shed, whistling "Horrible Hecuba". The men enter the shed and arrange their things along the stage right wall as they continue to whistle.*)

NARRATOR: When they got there they put their skins in a corner and started to prepare for dinner. Then they went to find kindling, berries, and corn for cooking.

(*The men cross down left out of sight of the audience.* HECUBA *moves upstage to platform on stage left.*)

HECUBA:
>Hecuba is a mean old witch
>With a heart of stone and a bag
> of tricks
>To trick ya.
>
>She'll pretend to be nice as pie
>But if you look in her evil eye
>She'll fix ya.
>
>So hunters, take care
>Beware
>Of heartless, hateful, horrible
> Hecuba

(*During song,* HECUBA *has crossed up to center stage. After her song* MATHEW *enters, whistling, "If I Had"*)

NARRATOR: The first to come back was Mathew, with an armful of kindling. (MATHEW *mimes building a fire and putting his things away, etc.*) After he built a fire, he put his venison on to cook. (HECUBA *moves down right on the ramp.)* In a few minutes, somebody knocked at the door . . . *(She knocks; MATHEW is startled.)*

MATHEW: Who's there?

HECUBA: I'm an old woman. I'm tired and cold. Could you give me shelter until morning? *(MATHEW crosses to face HECUBA.)*

MATHEW: You can come in and wait until the others come back and see what they say. *(He lets her in. She crosses in front of him, turns upstage, and sits on the step, saying,)*

HECUBA: Thank you, thank you. *(MATHEW crosses, stands over fire as he turns venison. He sings:)*

MATHEW:
If I had a horseshoe
I would trade it for a walking
    stick
And when Mary Lou came
    'round
I'd strut around with it . . . she'd
    say
Ooooooh what a splendid fella
So positively neat
He's such a well-dressed fella
Him I'd like to meet

HECUBA: What are you cooking?

MATHEW: Venison. *(Turns upstage and holds up the venison crossing up to the witch.)* See?

HECUBA: Oh, honey is very good on venison. I just happen to have some with me. Won't you try some? *(She pours.)*

MATHEW: Thank you.

(He begins to eat as HECUBA moves to centerstage and sings to audience, THEY WERE WARNED.)

HECUBA:
The honey will taste sweet but I
    put a
Potion in it
That will knock him cold in a
    minute
And while he's lying there
With his feet stuck in the air
I'll relieve him of his valuables.

HECUBA (con't.)
(*He falls out of sight behind stage right curtain. She follows, then sticks her head out to sing:*)

> It's not my fault, it's his own
> fault
> He was warned, he was warned,
> he was warned.
>
> It's not my fault, it's his own
> fault,
> He was warned, he was warned,
> he was warned.

(*During the last four lines, HECUBA robs him, then runs out of the house. Then EPHRAM enters, whistling IF I HAD A HORSESHOE.*)

NARRATOR: By and by Ephram came along; he put his venison on to cook. (*Notices fire, mimes putting his things away and cooking.*) In a few minutes somebody knocked at the door.

EPHRAM: Who's there?

HECUBA: I'm an old woman. I'm tired and cold. Could you give me shelter until morning?

EPHRAM: You can come in and wait until the others come back and see what they say. (*He lets her in.*)

HECUBA: Thank you, thank you. (*Crosses in front of him, then sits upstage*).

EPHRAM: (*Moves back to the fire to cook and begins to sing;*)

> If I had a wagon
> I would trade it for a famous
> book
> And when Mary Lou came
> 'round
> I'd let her have a look ... she'd
> say
> My what a well-read fella
> So learned and so smart
> He's such a brilliant fella
> He can have my heart

HECUBA: What are you cooking?

EPHRAM: Venison ... (*He holds it up.*) ... see?

HECUBA: (*Crossing down to him.*) ... Honey is very good on venison.

I just happen to have some with me. Won't you try some? (*She pours some on, then sings.*)

> His eyes are going to roll, to the
>   back of
> His hard head
> As he falls to the ground as if
>   dead
> And while he's in a trance
> I will have a chance
> To relieve him of all his
>   possessions

(*He falls in the same place as* MATHEW. *She follows and again puts her head out to sing.*)

> It's not my fault, it's his own
>   fault;
> After all they were warned, they
>   were warned
> It's not my fault, it's their own
>   fault
> They were warned, they were
>   warned, they were warned

(*She robs them, runs out, upstage center, and* CROESUS *enters stage left.*)

NARRATOR: By and by, Croesus came back. (*He crosses to stage right platform.*) He saw the fire and wondered where his friends went after they ate. (*He shows his puzzlement.*) And he put his venison on to cook. Directly along came the old woman again. She knocked.

CROESUS: Who's there?

HECUBA: I'm an old woman and I'm tired and cold. Can't I come in and sit with you until daybreak?

CROESUS: (*Crossing to "door."*) If your face is clean you can come in. If it ain't you can stay out, 'cause I'm getting ready to eat and I don't want no dirty-faced folk hanging about.

HECUBA: Oh, look, look for yourself, my face is clean. (*He peers out at her.*)

HECUBA: Thank you, thank you. (*She enters and sits upstage.*)

CROESUS: (CROESUS *goes back to the fire, thinks about her a minute, shrugs, and sings:*)

Croesus (con't.)

> If I had a pig's foot
> I would trade it for a chicken
>   delight
> And when Mary Lou came
>   'round
> I'd offer her a bite—she'd say,
> Oh, what a kind sweet fella
> Such generosity
> He's such a practical fella
> He's the one for me

Hecuba: Don't you need something to sweeten up your meal?

Croesus: No, I don't want nothin'!

Hecuba: That meat would taste mighty good with some honey on it. (*Crosses to where he is cooking.*) I have some and I'd be glad to share it with you. (*She tries to put some on his meat, but Croesus stops her.*)

Croesus: Listen, woman (*Forcing her back to the steps.*), I told you I don't want no honey on my food. I like it just the way it came off the bone.

Hecuba: All right. (*Shrinks back. Croesus starts downstage, stops to think, then sings to the audience:*)

Croesus: AHA

> Something's smelling mighty
>   funny
> Why does she insist on giving
>   me honey?
> Aha! O-ho!
> She thinks I don't know
> She's that witch which I've been
>   warned about
> That witch for which I'd better
>   watch out
> Aha, I see
> She's out to get me
> Well, she'd better think and
>   think again
> If she thinks I'll let her do me in
> She'll try to win our confidence
>   then fleece us
> Well, she'll soon see she's not as
>   smart as
> Croesus . . . is

(He crosses right near the wall, doing some business with his "supplies." HECUBA then crosses down to try to put honey on his venison, but he grabs her. He throws her down center on ramp.)

CROESUS: Aha! Oho! You think I don't
                        know
                You're that witch which I've
                        been
                Warned about
                That witch for which I'd better
                        watch out.

HECUBA: Please, please. I'm just a poor old woman! Would you hurt a poor old woman?

CROESUS: I know who you are, Hecuba! What have you done with my friends? Where are my friends? Where's Mathew? Where's Ephram?

HECUBA: Please, please, I'll tell you. I'm an old woman *(He grabs her again.)* . . . All right, your friends *(She crosses up right.)* . . . Ephram, Mathew! *(Moves her hand magically to release the spell, and they enter.)*

CROESUS: You still need to be taught a lesson. *(CROESUS tosses her across the stage; the men all chase her.)*

HECUBA: Stop! *(They freeze.)* I'll give you a magic treasure that'll help you out of mighty tight places. This *(The water dancer enters from stage right.)* . . . is magic water. Drop it on the ground and say, "Grow, water, grow!" In two minutes a river will rise that will be so long, so wide, so deep, you can't get around it, you can't swim over it, you can't wade across it. And this *(Corn dancer enters from stage left.)* . . . is a grain of corn. Drop it on the ground and say, "Grow, corn, grow!" In two minutes a field of corn will spring up that will be so long, so thick, so tall, you can't get around it, you can't get over it, you can't go through it. And this *(Mountain dancers enter from upstage center.)* . . . is a clod of mud. Drop it on the ground and say, "Grow, clay, grow!" and in two minutes a mountain will rise up that will be so wide, so rough, so steep that you can't get around it, you can't climb up it, and you can't get over it. And here *(Tree dancers enter and go to center stage.)* . . . is an acorn. Drop it on the ground and say, "Grow, acorn, grow!" In two minutes an oak tree will grow that will obey the one that planted it. It will do anything you ask except walk, 'cause it can't walk. So now you have water, corn, a mountain, and a magic tree. *(Sung)* . . . NOW, AIN'T THAT WORTH HAVING?

COMPANY: *(Song)* *(HECUBA exits.)*

COMPANY (con't.)

SO HIGH, SO WIDE, SO DEEP

So long, so wide, so deep
You can't get around it, you
    can't swim over it,
You can't wade across it, no, no,
    no.
You can't get around it, you
    can't swim over it,
You can't wade across it, no, no,
    no.
So long, so thick, so tall
You can't get around it, you
    can't get through it,
You can't get over it, no, no, no,
You can't get around it, you
    can't get through it,
You can't get over it, no, no, no,
So wide, so rough, so steep
You can't get around it, you
    can't climb up it,
You can't get over it, no, no, no.
You can't get around it, you
    can't climb up it,
You can't get over it, no, no, no.

(The hunters move off stage into the audience.)

DANCE: So Long, So Wide

THREE MEN: (While moving onto, across, and off stage again.)

So long
You can't get around it
So wide
You can't swim across it
So deep
You can't wade across it
So long
You can't get around it
So thick
You can't get through it
So tall
You can't get over it
So wide
You can't get around it
So rough
You can't climb up it

So steep
You can't get over it

(They exit upstage left to musical fade.)

NARRATOR: *(Enters from upstage left and stands on the stage right platform.)* The next day, as you see, they picked up their belongings and started their long journey home. By and by, they got lost in the thick woods. *(The three enter stage left and cross to the stage right platform.)* They kept on until they came to a little house with a light in it. They knocked and a lady came to the door and said . . .

(They all knock to the rhythm of her change from HECUBA *to a seductress.)*

HECUBA: Hi, guys. *(Offers hand. They are smitten.)*

CROESUS: Good evening, ma'am. We're lost.

EPHRAM: But I think we've found the way.

CROESUS: I wonder if you could tell us the way . . . to the city.

HECUBA: Come in, come in. The brothers are going to the city early in the morning. You might as well stay here and go with them. *(They enter and walk around her, humming,* YOU CAN DO WHAT YOU WANNA DO.*)* Would you like something to drink?

THREE MEN: Yes, ma'am. *(They all sit down, except* EPHRAM.*)*

HECUBA: Sit down! *(To* EPHRAM.*)*

(While she gives them food and drink, she sings:)

> They are mighty handsome
>   wolves
> Oh, but if they only knew
> What this clever little fox is
>   going to do
> After supper when they rest
> I'll be feathering my nest
> As I divest them of their lives
>   and belongings . . .
>
> It's not my fault
> It's their own fault
> After all, they were warned,
>   they were warned
>
> It's not my fault
> It's their own fault

HECUBA (con't.)

> They were warned, they were
> warned, they were warned.

(HECUBA blows each one a kiss then exits. All the men start to follow her while whistling and wolf howling, etc. They turn back toward downstage center, then all sing their own verse of IF I HAD, separately, and sing the final verse together, crossing to stage left positions. During this time the brothers enter.)

MATHEW: (Crossing onto the stage left platform.)

> If I had a horseshoe
> I would trade it for a walking
>   stick
> And when Mary Lou came
>   'round
> I'd strut around with it—she'd
>   say
> Oooooh what a splendid fella
> So positively neat
> He's such a well-dressed fella
> Him I'd like to meet

EPHRAM: (Crossing, too.)

> If I had a wagon
> I would trade it for a famous
>   book
> And when Mary Lou came
>   'round
> I'd let her have a look—she'd
>   say
> My what a well-read fella
> So learned and so smart
> He's such a brilliant fella
> He can have my heart

CROESUS:

> If I had a pig's foot
> I would trade it for a chicken
>   delight
> And when Mary Lou came
>   'round
> I'd offer her a bite . . . she'd say
> Oh, what a kind, sweet fella
> Such generosity
> He's such a practical fella
> He's the one for me

ALL THREE MEN: (*Crossing back to the stage right platform.*)

> If I had a thumbtack
> I would trade it for some Elmer's
>   glue
> And when Mary Lou came
>   'round
> She'd stick to you-know-who
> And I'd say
> Oh, what a lucky fella
> Fortunate as can be
> I'm such a happy fella
> Mary Lou is stuck on me . . .

(*The men lie down to sleep, repeating the last line more and more softly until they doze off.*)

NARRATOR: She had told them after supper that night that they all had to sleep in the same bed. And that the brothers had to sleep in the same room in another bed, for there was very little room. After they had all gone to sleep, she eased into the room carrying red and green caps. Very carefully she put the red nightcaps on Croesus and his friends and the green nightcaps on the heads of the brothers, so that, later that night, when she came back to murder them, she would know who was who.

HECUBA:

> The tree of life has fruit ripe for
>   the picking
> If you want a share you've got to
>   be firm.
> Catching an extra forty winks is
>   easy
> But the early bird is out there
>   catching the worm,
>
> You can get what you wanna
>   get,
> You can go where you wanna
>   go,
> You can do what you wanna do,
> By doing it.

(*CROESUS, suspicious from the start, opens one eye then sits up slowly and starts to sing:*)

CROESUS:

> Things are looking kinda shady
> Something is familiar about that
>   lady . . .

CROESUS (*con't.*)

> Aha! Oh wow!
> I'm on to her now
> She's that same old witch we
>   met before
> And she's up to her same old
>   tricks once more
>
> Aha! Oh yes,
> Unless I miss my guess
> She will try to kill us in our beds
> By the caps we're wearing on
>   our heads

(*MATHEW and EPHRAM wake and slowly realize what is happening. They get up.*)

> She thinks we're fooled by the
>   nice way
> That she treats us
> But I'll show her she can't think
>   as fast as
> Croesus can!

(*During the rest of the song, the three switch caps with the brothers and mime stuffing their beds.*)

ALL THREE MEN:

> Aha! Oh wow!
> We're on to her now
> She's that same old witch we
>   met before
> And she's up to her same old
>   tricks once more
>
> Aha! Oh yes!
> Unless we miss our guess
> She will try to kill us in our beds
> By the caps we're wearing on
>   our heads
> She thinks we're fooled by the
>   nice way that she treats us

CROESUS:

> But we'll show her she can't
>   think as fast
> As Croe...

MATHEW and EPHRAM: ... sus

CROESUS: Sus can!

NARRATOR: And they took their pillows and stuffed them into their beds as if they were still there.

(*MATHEW and EPHRAM mime stuffing while CROESUS explains, then CROESUS stuffs his bed and they exit upstage right.*)

NARRATOR: Directly along, the Lady eased in. When she saw the hats, she thought they had changed beds. So she tipped to the bed where the red caps were, pulled out a great club, and knocked them on the heads. Then she went to the other bed. (*Cross to stage left platform.*)

HECUBA: Get up from there, you lazy bones. Do you think I hired you to lay up and sleep? Get up and carry these men out of here.

(*CROESUS and pals jump out from their hiding place and surround HECUBA, snap their fingers, and sing:*)

ALL THREE MEN: (*Circling HECUBA.*)

> When you're out to do another
> in
> Look out you don't burst your
> balloon with
> Your own pin.
> While you're trying to block my
> path
> Someone else may get the last
> laugh on you,
>
> Be careful when you step on
> toes
> Or you may trip yourself,
> You could get hit in the back
> While throwing stones at
> someone else . . .
>
> While you're busy digging other
> graves
> Look out or the dirt might fly
> back in your face
> You may double-cross with
> unconcern
> But the evil that you do will
> turn on you.

(*They grab HECUBA, tie her up, and tape her mouth.*)

> Calling names and hurting folks
> I can live without it,

ALL THREE MEN (con't.)

>Before you try to cut my throat
>Think about it!
>
>While you're busy digging other graves
>Look out or the dirt might fly back in your face
>You can double-cross with unconcern
>But the evil that you do will turn on you.

(They exit. HECUBA manages to untie herself and revive the brothers.)

HECUBA: Hellion!
　　　　Heathen!
　　　　Horrid!

(They jump up, cross downstage center, and face upstage. HECUBA runs upstage center.)

HECUBA: After them!

(They simulate running and cross upstage center, then turn stage left and exit. The hunters enter from behind the stage left curtain and, simulating running, cross straight downstage, and run in place. The narrator enters behind them, running in place as HECUBA.)

NARRATOR: Croesus was really flying high (The three men enter from the stage left curtain.), but when he looked back, the witch was within five feet of him. He thought:

CROESUS: Aha, the magic treasure! (CROESUS runs to stage left edge of stage right platform at steps, throws corn down.) Grow, corn, grow!

DANCERS: Dance of the Corn

NARRATOR: As you saw, the witch was surprised to see the corn and tried to ride through, but it was too thick. She tried to get around it, but it was too long and too wide, so she went home to get an axe to cut it down. While she was doing that, CROESUS was making time. But she was pretty swift and it didn't take her long.

(CROESUS drops the water.)

CROESUS: Grow, water, grow!

DANCERS: Dance of the Water

NARRATOR: As you saw, she was able to swim out of it. When Croesus looked back, Hecuba was within ten feet of him. She took an axe from her side and threw it.

(*MATHEW and EPHRAM dodge but CROESUS catches it and throws it back at her.*)

CROESUS: Holy smoke!

EPHRAM: Holy mackerel!

MATHEW: Holy cow!

(*CROESUS throws the mud on the ground.*)

CROESUS: Grow, clay, grow!

DANCERS: Dance of the Mountain

NARRATOR: As you saw, she took out her axe and was able to dig a hole through the middle of the mountain. She was determined to get Croesus and the deerskin. When Croesus saw her coming, he dropped the acorn to the ground.

(*He drops it.*)

CROESUS: Grow, acorn, grow! (*The dancers line up on the center ramp, crouched down. They straighten slowly, bringing their arms out straight from their sides, or higher.*)

NARRATOR: And the tree began to grow, and Croesus climbed to the top. (*He climbs by walking up the ramp and pushing or pulling their arms out of his way.*) Hecuba shook the tree (*Mimes shaking tree*), but he wouldn't fall, so she took her axe and began to chop the tree (*Mimes chopping.*) and chopped and chopped at the tree. The tree commenced to shake and the chips commenced to fly. The tree was ready to fall, when Croesus said ...

CROESUS: Chips, fly back to your places.

NARRATOR: Hecuba was mighty surprised to see the chips jump off the ground and get back in the tree. Hecuba got so mad, she began to throw rocks up at the tree (*Mimes throwing rocks as CROESUS sneaks off the upstage side of the tree.*), but the leaves were so thick she couldn't hit Croesus. Then she began to cut again. (*Mimes chopping.*) The tree was almost ready to fall when Croesus said:

CROESUS: Obey Croesus.

MATHEW: (*Enters*) Destroy the Hag.

EPHRAM: (*Enters*) Destroy the Witch.

THREE MEN: Destroy Hecuba!

(Tree falls on HECUBA.)

(As the dust settles and the lights fade down, the men sing while moving downstage, picking up belongings and walking upstage center.)

THREE MEN:

While you're busy digging other
    graves
Look out or the dirt might fly
    back in your face
You may double-cross with
    unconcern
But the evil that you do will
    turn on you.

(The NARRATOR rises and gently wakes all of the dancers.)

NARRATOR: The End.

(The lights fade to black and then come up brightly on the company as they sing:)

COMPANY:
                        FINALE

No use sitting, waiting for
    something to happen
Sitting, twiddling your fingers
    and your toes,
You can be out making your
    own thing happen
Instead of sitting at home
    scratching your nose.

You can get what you wanna
    get
You can go where you wanna
    go
You can do what you wanna do
By doing it

Today will be yesterday
    tomorrow
If you want to sit around and
    wait

You will just be hungrier
　　tomorrow
And you won't have any grits to
　　put on your plate.

(*The production number progresses to a curtain call, and as the last company members leave the stage, the lights fade to black.*)

END OF PLAY

Hansel and Gretel
(in the 1980s)

Cast
(in order of appearance)

WILMA the Witch

TROLL the Mold

SAM the FROG

IRMA Wolfgang

HANSEL Wolfgang

GRETEL Wolfgang

HERMAN Wolfgang

Oakey the TREE

CLARABIRD

SARA the Squirrel

CYNTHIA the Cockatoo

Pearlie, OWL No. 1

Mimic, OWL No. 2

FLORENCE

Characters may be played by adults and/or by children ranging in ages from 10–17 years.

Act One

(House is half-dark. Suddenly, we hear forest noises. DANCE OF ANIMALS in audience area. Forest scene builds. The WITCH enters, riding on TROLL's (her servant) back. All animals scatter. Blackout.)

WITCH: I've got to find me some kids. I'm starving to death, Troll. Where are they? I've been looking everywhere. Come on, Troll, get a move on. *(She laughs, "witchstyle," and exits.)*

FROG: Wow, that was close. *(As he races through the house, leaping and yelling.)* Can't seem to catch those flies anymore. Gosh, darn it, wish I had a fly swatter. This leaping around all day is getting me crazy. *(Swats a couple of times more; suddenly he sees the audience. Very apologetically.)* Oh, good grief, I'm so sorry, I didn't see you out there. I get so involved in getting these flies that I hardly know where I am sometimes. *(Straightens himself, becomes dignified.)* You're obviously here to hear about Hansel and Gretel. They're really nice kids who got a raw deal. We know them well because they sometimes come out here in the forest and play with us. As a matter of fact, the latest word on them is that their stepmother—man, is she awful—just wants old man Wolfgang—that's the father—to put them out. She's a real ditso, that one.

(We hear a scream from offstage.)

IRMA: This place is a mess. I can't stand it anymore—get rid of those kids.

FROG: Oh, brother, there she goes again. Good ole' Irma. Let me tell you about her.

GOOD OLD IRMA

Good old Irma, good old Irma,
You'd think she was the soul of daintiness
But she never cleans the house then blames the
children for the mess. That's good old Irma.
She likes to lie around all day and grumble and groan,
When she's not doing that she's on the telephone.

With good old Florence, good old Florence,
She's Irma's bosom friend and that's not odd

FROG (con't.)
'Cause the two are so alike they're just like
two peas in a pod, Flo and Irma.

Good old Irma, handing out orders like a queen,
Good old Royal Highness, how come you act so doggone mean?

(Spoken) All those two ever do is drink coffee, talk on the phone, and go to lunches. Old Wolfgang is out slaving away all day and what does he come home to?

To good Old Irma, good old Irma,
Who greets him at the door with her complaints,
To hear her talk you'd think that little
kids should all be saints, that's good old Irma.
As for the kids, Hansel and Gretel, you can be sure
They get the chores while Irma gets a manicure.

Good old Irma, handing out orders like a queen,
Good Old Royal Highness, how come you act so doggone mean?

At any rate, let me give you a birdseye view of life in good ole' Tannerstown, the garden state of the Ukraine. (Note: You may substitute any country desired.)

(Curtain opens. Scene is home of HANSEL and GRETEL's livingroom. HANSEL and GRETEL are scrubbing the floor; STEPMOTHER is filing her nails, lounging on the couch.)

FROG: Well, as you can see, we have a very happy home here . . .

(HANSEL and GRETEL look at him angrily.)

. . . or at least someone's happy

(STEPMOTHER smiles at FROG and resumes nail filing. FROG looks at his watch.)

Oh, oh, time for old man Wolgang to come home.

(Stepping noises and coughing are heard offstage.)

HERMAN: (Coughing as he enters, looking very sad and worn out.) Hello, everybody.

(HANSEL and GRETEL rush to him. IRMA stops them. She puts on an apron.)

IRMA: Just a minute, take your places.

(They stand behind her, HANSEL first, then GRETEL. IRMA extends her hand and WOLFGANG kisses it. She then turns and goes to the couch to *pretend she's exhausted. At that point, HANSEL and GRETEL run and hug WOLFGANG as IRMA turns around. They pretend to curtsy instead.)*

HANSEL and GRETEL: Good evening, Father.

WOLFGANG: Good evening, children. How was your day?

(The children start to speak, but IRMA interrupts.)

IRMA: Oh, I had the most exhausting day. I cleaned and cleaned and cooked and cooked. I'm so exhausted and these kids, they're just useless. You must talk to them.

(HANSEL and GRETEL look at each other, about to protest to their father. IRMA interrupts again.)

IRMA: They just don't help me at all. They've been doing that floor for three hours.

HANSEL: But you told us to do it three times.

GRETEL: And my hands hurt.

(The children are almost crying. Their father starts to protest.)

IRMA: Don't you say a word, Herman. I refuse to be disputed. Children, go to your room now!

(The children move reluctantly. As they exit, IRMA continues.)

IRMA: I tell you, Herman, this has become so hard for me. You know I'm not well... with all this cleaning and cleaning and cooking and cooking I just can't seem to get through the day. Everything I tell those kids they just refuse to do, or they take so long to do it.

HERMAN: I know, dear, I know. I'll... I'll speak to them.

IRMA: You'll speak to them? *You'll* speak to them? Really, Herman, they don't listen to anybody, and especially you. You're so... so... so easy with them. You need to be firmer, Herman. That Hansel, he has so much mouth. You need to be firmer, Herman. Kids need a strong hand.

CHILDREN NEED DISCIPLINE

It's time for you to take control,
Forget about Dr. Spock,
You let 'em have their way
And that's why today
We've got the worst kids on the block.
Children need discipline

IRMA (con't.)
Like a wild horse needs a rope,
Instead of ho-ho-hoing like Santa Claus
You gotta let 'em know who's boss.

It's time you laid it on the line
And put your big foot down hard,
I was a kid once, too,
I know what kids will do,
You give 'em a foot they'll take a yard.

Children need discipline
Like a wild horse needs a rope,
Instead of ho-ho-hoing like Santa Claus .
You gotta let 'em know who's boss.

You gotta keep 'em hoppin' and keep 'em moppin'
If you wanna keep 'em in their places,
You gotta be on your guard and disregard
Those sweet angel faces.

Children need discipline
Like a wild horse needs a rope,
Instead of ho-ho-hoing like Santa Claus
You gotta let 'em know who's boss!

HERMAN: (*Sadly*) Yes, dear, you're probably right. I'll ... I'll be strong. I promise.

IRMA: (*Pats him on the head.*) Good boy, Herman. (*Stretches*) I've been working so hard all day, I think I'll take a nap. (*Starts to go.*)

HERMAN: But, dear, isn't there any dinner?

IRMA: Dinner? Oh, yes, well I had lunch today with Florence, so I'm not hungry—but there's food in the ice box.

HERMAN: Irma, please, just a moment. I have something to tell you.

IRMA: Oh, Herman, can't it wait?

HERMAN: I'm afraid it's waited long enough. Please, Irma, come and sit down.

IRMA: Oh, all right, if you insist. (*She sits.*)

HERMAN: (*Starts reluctantly*) Well, you see Irma, it's like this. I've been going out every day dressed as if I've been going to work when actually I've been looking for work.

IRMA: (*Becoming hysterical*) What do you mean—looking for work? You have a job.

HERMAN: I had a job, Irma.

IRMA: What?

HERMAN: I was fired two weeks ago. They're laying off down at the plant and I got the axe.

IRMA: You got the axe? You got the axe? (*Starts to cry.*) Herman, I can't believe what you're saying. What are we going to do?

HERMAN: Now, now, dear, don't cry. I'll find something else.

IRMA: When?

HERMAN: Soon, soon I hope.

IRMA: (*Crying loudly*) Oh, Herman, what are we going to do?

(*They exit. Lights fade down on stage and back to FROG.*)

FROG: Well, good ole' Herman got the axe. What'll you know about that. He's such a sweet guy, too. (*Hears HANSEL and GRETEL whispering as they enter the Forest Area.*)

OAKEY THE TREE: Okay, everyone, come on, I've got the ball. (*All animals enter and form separate teams.*)

FROG: Hey, what's going on out there?

(*Animals and HANSEL and GRETEL are playing volleyball.*)

HANSEL: Don't worry, Sam. We're just having a little game of volleyball.

(*General ad libs: 'Throw the ball!'; 'Hey, watch out!'; 'Over here!'; 'I got it!'; etc.*)

FROG: Say, Hansel, Gretel, come over here. I've got something to tell you.

HANSEL: Hang on everybody, we'll be back in a minute. Come on, Gretel.

(*They cross down to FROG.*)

HANSEL: What's up, Sam?

FROG: I just overheard your father tell your stepmother he's been fired.

HANSEL and GRETEL and Animals: Fired!

FROG: Yep! He's been out of work for two weeks.

HANSEL: But we thought he was working.

GRETEL: He was going out every day.

FROG: Well, you see, he's just been going out looking for work every day. But hasn't found anything yet.

GRETEL: Oh, Hansel, what does this mean? You know Irma doesn't like us. I overheard her talking to Florence about putting us in a foster home.

HANSEL: Come on, Gretel, now don't get excited. Maybe he'll find something soon.

(*Lights halfway up on stage area—see* IRMA *in nightgown.*)

IRMA: What's that noise out there? Who's out there?

(*She listens. Animals,* FROG, HANSEL, *and* GRETEL *run their respective ways—*FROG *into audience area,* HANSEL *and* GRETEL *back into the house through the side door.*)

Goodness, I must be hearing things. I'm just so nervous. Herman is such a dumbbell—losing his job. (*Goes to make a phone call.*) What am I going to do? What am I going to do? I know we can get rid of the kids. That will save a small fortune. They eat too much, anyway. Yes, that's what I'll do, and I'll get Florence to help me. (*At phone.*) Hello, Florence. Oh, I'm sorry, I didn't mean to wake you. Florence, listen. I've got to talk to somebody. Yes, I know it's late, dear, but can you come over tomorrow for coffee? Yes, dear, around 10:00—yes, that'll be fine. Uh huh, yes I know you have a hair appointment at 12:00—no, dear, this won't take long. Yes, fine, I'll see you then. (*She exits.*)

FROG: (*Creeps toward stage with* OWL NO. 1) Did you hear that, Pearlie?

OWL NO. 1: I sure did, Sam. We can't let her harm Hansel and Gretel. They're our friends. What shall we do?

FROG: Heck if I know. I'm sure ole' Wolfgang won't throw them out.

OWL NO. 1: How do you know? He's a pretty weak fellow.

(*Mimic,* OWL NO. 2, *appears, repeating.*)

OWL NO. 2: He's a pretty weak fellow.

OWL NO. 1: Will you be quiet and stop following me?

OWL NO. 2: Will you be quiet and stop following me?

OWL NO. 1: Just once, just once I wish I could go somewhere without you.

OWL NO. 2: (*Starts to repeat.*) Just once ...

FROG: (*Stops her. Places his hand over her mouth while* OWL NO. 2 *is repeating the words.*) Hold on a minute, we've got things to do. We've got to be sure no harm will come to Hansel and Gretel.

OWL NO. 1: Because they're our friends and we love them.

OWL NO. 2: Because they're our friends and we love them.

OWL NO. 1: And what are friends for if we can't help?

OWL NO. 2: And what are friends for if we can't help?

(OWL *No. 1 rolls eyes at* OWL *No. 2.*)

FROG: Yeah, what are friends for.

(*Song and Dance:—Friendship Routine*)

FRIENDSHIP

A Friend	Is there in a pinch
"	Never runs from trouble
"	When you're in a fix
"	Is there on the double
"	Will not let you down
"	When you're in a pickle
"	If he's got a dime
"	You've got a nickle.
	Friendship, friendship
	There's no better ship than friendship.
A Friend	Is there when it rains
"	Not just when it's sunny
"	Will laugh at your jokes
"	Even though they're not funny,
"	Is there when you lose
"	Not only when you're winning
"	When you're all tied up
"	Will go an extra inning.
	Friendship, friendship
	There's no better ship than friendship
	There are tall ships and small ships
	And scholarships and fellowships
	And every other kind of ship—but
	Friendship, friendship
	There's no better ship than

FROG (con't.)

(Modulate)   Friendship, Friendship
             There's no better ship than friendship

(Song and dance end. We hear alarm clock ringing, back on stage; house area.)

FROG: Hey, it's daylight already. Let's go over to my pad and figure out how we can help Hansel and Gretel.

OWL No. 1: Okay, Sam.

OWL No. 2: Okay, Sam.

OWL No. 1: Shut up and come on.

OWL No. 2: Shut up . . .

FROG: Okay, okay let's go.

(They exit to pad in forest area.)

IRMA: (Dressed in robe, enters, yelling.) All right, all right, everybody out.

(HANSEL and GRETEL run through, putting on coats and hats, leaving with lunches and books. IRMA snatches lunch from GRETEL.)

IRMA: Share your brother's lunch. We have to be thrifty. Food is scarce these days.

(They look at each other. GRETEL starts to protest; HANSEL pulls her on.)

HANSEL: Come on, Gretel, it's OK. I'm never hungry at lunchtime anyway.

GRETEL: Yes, you are. You're always eating.

HANSEL: It's OK, really, come on.

(They leave.)

IRMA: Dumb kids. (Yells off stage.) Herman, let's go.

HERMAN: (Entering) Yes, Irma, I'm ready to go.

IRMA: (Hands him several newspapers.) There are thousands of jobs, Herman. I've checked these newspapers, now get a move on. (Pushes him out the door.) Good, now I can get on with my plans. (Doorbell rings) Oh, that must be Florence. (She goes to and opens the door.) Florence, hello, do come in. (They kiss and hug.)

FLORENCE: (*Dressed very well*) Irma, my dear, whatever is wrong with you? You sounded so disturbed last night. Darling, you must be calm. Don't let things upset you so much.

IRMA: Florence, Herman lost his job.

FLORENCE: (*Hysterical*) What! Irma, you can't be serious. Darling, I was depending on you to lend me the money for my new car.

IRMA: Well, I'm afraid that's out. My biggest problem is that I've taken all of the money out of the savings account to buy a fur coat and other things. He doesn't know it because I handle all of the bills.

FLORENCE: Well, what are you going to do?

IRMA: I've got to get rid of those kids. That could save us a great deal.

FLORENCE: Oh, yes, darling. Kids are a drag. All they ever do is eat, sleep, get sick, and grow. It's that growing that's so expensive.

IRMA: Yes, I know...and I can't stand all of their school problems...so boring.

FLORENCE: How are you going to get rid of them?

IRMA: Well, I thought maybe I could convince Herman to place them in a foster home for a while until he finds a job.

FLORENCE: Oh, Irma, good ole' Herm adores those children. He'll never do it.

IRMA: Florence, yes he will. Do you remember that potion Mrs. Ouspenskia gave us last year at the Halloween Party? Well, she said that it can really cast a spell on anyone who takes it. I'm going to give it to Herman and then convince him to get rid of the kids.

FLORENCE: Mrs. Ouspenskia. Oh, yes, the old lady with the giant earrings who kept talking about werewolves and things.

IRMA: Yes, that one. Well, she said that the potion can really cast a spell on anyone who takes it. I'm going to give it to Herman and then convince him to get rid of the kids.

FLORENCE: Well, darling, if she said it could cast a spell then it probably can. She was very weird, but never mind her, darling. I love the idea. Now, when are you planning on serving up the goodies?

IRMA: Now, here's where you come in. Later this afternoon Herman will probably come home around 2:00 for lunch. You come over in your gypsy costume, I'll wear mine, and we'll serve him some tea with the potion in it. Once he's asleep we'll do the voodoo ceremony Mrs. Ouspenskia taught us. Here's the paper with the words on it.

FLORENCE: Herman Herman
                  Hear this sermon

IRMA: No, no, darling, it goes like this. (*She begins to read it as if she's casting a spell.*)

                  Herman, Herman
                  Hear this sermon

FLORENCE: Oh, yes, now I remember how she did it.

FLORENCE and IRMA: (*Read*)

                  Herman, Herman
                  Hear this sermon
                  The children
                  You know
                  They must go
                  Food is scarce
                  The cupboard is clean
                  If we stay this way
                  We'll all be lean
                  Herman, Herman
                  Hear this sermon.

FLORENCE: Oh, Irma, this is delightful. I can't wait. (*Looks at her watch.*) Oh, darling, I must run now. My hair appointment is in fifteen minutes.

IRMA: Well, I think I'll take my morning nap.

(*She exits. Lights fade on stage, up on FROG.*)

FROG: Well, now that just beats all. Irma has really flipped her wig for sure. The lady's a nut.

OWL NO. 1: Well, we've got to help Hansel and Gretel.

OWL NO. 2: We've got to help Hansel and Gretel.

(*OWL NO. 1, as always, is annoyed by OWL NO. 2's repetition.*)

FROG: Yeah, you're right. First thing, we've got to let them know what Irma is up to.

Owl No. 1: How do we do that?

Owl No. 2: How do we do that?

Frog: What time do they get home from school?

Owl No. 1: About 3:30.

Owl No. 2: About 3:30.

Frog: Well, we've got to get them before they get home. What time is it now?

Owl No. 1: (*Looks at sky*) It's about eleven o'clock.

Owl No. 2: (*Repeats action*) It's about eleven o'clock.

Frog: Now, listen up. We'll go to their school at recess time and mingle in the schoolyard until we find them and then we'll tell them what's going on.

Owl No. 1: But won't we look a little strange?

Owl No. 2: You will, I won't!

Owl No. 1: (*Angrily*) One of these days I'm going to break your wings.

Frog: Wait now...yeah, you're right. Listen, I'll sneak into Hansel's room and get some of his clothes and we can disguise ourselves. That way no one will notice we're different.

Owl No. 1: Good idea!

Owl No. 2: Good idea!

Frog: Stay here; this won't take long.

Owl No. 1: I hope not. We haven't much time.

Owl No. 2: I hope not...

Owl No. 1: (*Exasperated*) Okay, okay. Shut up!

(*Frog sneaks into side door of Hansel's house as Owls creep around outside.*)

Owl No. 1: This is making me nervous.

Owl No. 2: This is making me nervous.

Owl No. 1: Irma'll kill him if she sees him. She hates frogs.

(*Owl No. 2 starts to repeat and is cut off by Owl No. 1.*)

OWL NO. 1: And mimicking owls.

(OWL NO. 2 *places wings over mouth and starts to shake.* OWL NO. 1 *gets great pleasure out of seeing this.*)

FROG: (*Returns with jackets, hats, glasses*) Okay, here. Whew. Boy, that was close. Ole' Irma almost woke up from her nap.

(*They put on outfits and also try to act like tough guys.*)

FROG: Okay, okay, now remember, you're boys, so walk and talk like them. Let's go.

(*They exit through the house, acting like tough guys. Ad libs: "Cool it, man!" "Get down!" "Don't try it!", etc. All the while* OWL NO. 2 *continues to repeat what everyone says.*)

(*Lights up on stage area. Stage is empty. Offstage* FLORENCE *is banging at the door.*)

FLORENCE: Irma ... Irma, hurry open the door.

(IRMA *rushes onto the stage dressed in gypsy costume and carrying tea tray.*)

IRMA: Florence, come in. What's all the rush?

(FLORENCE *enters, dressed in a gypsy outfit.*)

FLORENCE: Well, people were passing by me, looking at me as if I were a nut or something. After all, darling, this isn't Halloween.

IRMA: Oh, Florence, you look marvelous. Now, I've got the tea ready with the sleeping potion in it. Come on, let's practice the ritual.

(*There is a dance routine first, then the ritual begins.*)

IRMA and FLORENCE: (*In gypsy-type voices*)

> Herman, Herman
> Hear this sermon
> The children
> You know
> They must go
> Food is scarce
> The cupboard is clean
> If we stay this way
> We'll all be lean
> Herman, Herman
> Hear this sermon.

IRMA: Oh, Florence, that's perfect. Wait a minute. (*She listens at the door.*) I think Herman's coming. Get the tea ready. (FLORENCE *pours the tea.*)

FLORENCE: Everything's set, darling!

(IRMA *opens the door.* HERMAN *looks puzzled because he was about to use his key.*)

IRMA: Oh, Herman, you're home so early.

(HERMAN *looks tired and forlorn.*)

HERMAN: Yes, dear, I didn't have much luck today. Oh, hello, Florence. Say, what are you two dressed up for?

IRMA: Oh . . . ah . . . we're trying on our costumes for the Charity Ball next week.

FLORENCE: Yes, we're going to be reading cards and crystal balls . . . you know, gypsy-type stuff.

HERMAN: Oh, yes, I forgot all about the Charity Ball.

IRMA: Well, Herman, why don't you have some tea to relax you?

HERMAN: Yes, that's a good idea. (*He sips some tea.*) This is very good. (*He continues to drink.*) You're right. This really relaxes me. (*He starts to yawn.*) Gosh, I really feel sleepy. I feel so sl . . . e . . . e . . . p . . . y. (*He falls off to sleep.*)

IRMA: Good. At last.

FLORENCE: Okay, where do we begin?

IRMA: From the beginning, of course.

(*They start the ritual. From the back of the house,* FROG, OWLS, HANSEL, *and* GRETEL *enter.*)

FROG: Hey, they've already started.

GRETEL: What are they doing? What are we going to do, Hansel? (*Slightly hysterical*) What are we going to do, Hansel?

(*The ritual continues.*)

HANSEL: Don't worry, I'll think of something.

FROG and OWLS: We'll think of something.

(*Ritual is done in dim light and slow motion.*)

IRMA: Okay, Florence, I think we can relax now. He's out cold.

FLORENCE: Thank goodness. I'm exhausted.

IRMA: Darling, did I show you my new dress I got at Gimbels, $150?

FLORENCE: (*Growing excitement*) No kidding! Where is it—what color?

IRMA: Purple, darling—right this way.

(*They exit into house area.*)

(*Lights come up on FROG, OWLS, and children.*)

OWL No. 1: I know—let's take them into the Twilight Zone.

OWL No. 2: The Twilight Zone.

FROG: What are they going to do there?

OWL No. 1: Well, until we can clear Herman's head with the anti-potion, Hansel and Gretel need a place to stay.

OWL No. 2: . . . a place to stay.

FROG: But suppose Wilma the Witch and her crew know we've got the kids in the Zone? She'll freak out. You know how she loves kid-ke-bob.

OWL No. 1: Yeah, that's true, but we'll have to take a chance. Look, Sam, you and I will have to mix the anti-potion and try to get it in Herman. Mimic, here, can take the kids to the Zone. (*Speaking to OWL No. 2.*) You think you can do that?

OWL No. 2: You think you can do that?

OWL No. 1: (*Yells*) Stop that and answer me!

OWL No. 2: (*Flies around*) All right, all right, I can do that.

FROG: Okay, that's settled. Let's get down to the herb valley and get the supplies for the anti-potion.

OWL No. 1: All right, now you kids get going and Sam and I will pick you up when the coast is clear. (*To OWL No. 2*) And make sure they're well taken care of.

(*OWL No. 1 and FROG leave.*)

OWL No. 2: Well taken care of. Well taken care of.

HANSEL: Well, which way do we go?

GRETEL: Oh, Hansel, I'm scared.

HANSEL: Don't worry, Gretel, if we can get Mimic to lead the way, I'm sure we'll be all right. Now, please, tell us which way we go.

OWL No. 2: Which way do we go? Which way do we go?

GRETEL: Maybe she doesn't know.

HANSEL: Good grief . . . what are we gonna do?

OWL No. 2: Okay, okay, now I remember. What are we gonna do? What are we gonna do? What we are gonna do is, close our eyes and spread our wings, my wings, your arms, and say—

(*Disco music*)

> Dishes and Wishes
> Clones and Clones
> Take us all to
> The Twilight Zone
> The Twilight Zone
> The Twilight Zone

(*The children repeat this. There is a lightning flash; music and animal noises persist. There is a ritualistic building of the forest, with dance movements and sounds, etc.*)

HANSEL: Wow, this place is fantastic!

GRETEL: It's even better than what Sam said it was. I could stay here forever.

HANSEL: Yeah, I feel the same way.

GRETEL: Except I would miss Father. He seems so lonely with Irma.

HANSEL: Yeah, she's a real . . . well, she's just an awful person.

TREE: (*In a Mae West-type voice*) Hi, kids, take a load off your feet and rest under my branches. I'm called Oakey, that's because I'm o-kay; you know what I mean.

(*She laughs sexily. HANSEL and GRETEL look at each other strangely.*)

HANSEL and GRETEL: Oh, yeah, thanks . . . we are kind of tired.

HANSEL: The trip here was rough.

GRETEL: I'm exhausted.

CLARABIRD: (*Flies around TREE and children.*) Merry Christmas, Merry Christmas . . . Happy New Year, Happy New Year! (*Hiccups; continues around TREE as if smashed from a New Year's Eve Party.*)

HANSEL: What's the matter with her?

GRETEL: She's acting rather strange.

TREE: Oh, don't mind her. She's still celebrating the New Year. She's been celebrating for a year now. She always is celebrating one thing or another. (*Yells to* CLARABIRD) Clarabird, say hello to Hansel and Gretel.

GRETEL: How did you know our names?

TREE: Darling, I know everything. (*Laughs sexily*) I read about you guys in a book.

(*Laughs again.* HANSEL *and* GRETEL *look at each·other, unsure of what she means.*)

TREE: Oh, oh, here comes Sara and Cynthia.

(SARA *the squirrel and* CYNTHIA *the cockatoo enter.*)

SARA: (*Always speaking as if she has nuts in her cheeks.*) Hi, kids, are you hungry? I've got plenty of food, plenty of food. (*Takes nuts out of her bags and gives them to kids. She is highly nervous and jerky. Drops nuts and anxiously tries to pick them up and hand them to the kids, making a worse mess.*) Oh, oh, I'm sorry, I'm sorry. Here, I can pick them up.

CYNTHIA: (*In high-pitched voice*) Oh, you drive me to distraction. You are such a nervous ninny. Here, get back and let me feed the kids.

SARA: No, no, I can do it, I can do it.

CYNTHIA: You cannot, you can't do anything but make a mess.

(*They continue to argue. The* TREE *shouts.*)

TREE: Hold it! Hold it! I'm getting a migraine from all this. Clara, do you have anything I can take?

CLARABIRD: Do I have anything, do I have anything? (*Searches through her pockets.*) No, I don't have anything . . . I don't have nothing. I don't have nothing but myself.

TREE: Oh, good grief, sometimes life can be so trying—

TREE'S LAMENT
(IS THAT ANY WAY TO TREAT A TREE?)

The rain comes down
And it drops on me,
A bird sits down on my branch
Then plops on me,
I ask you, Is that any way to treat a tree?

Then old Jack Frost
Puts the freeze on me,
A dog stops by, lifts his leg
And . . . on me,
I ask you, Is that any way to treat a tree?

Just look at me, I'm gorgeous.
The finest of nature's greenery,
Decked out from limb to leaf,
I'm a credit, to the scenery.

Then here you come
Making my head ache,
And you've got no aspirin
For me to take. I ask you
Is that any way to treat a gorgeous tree like me?
Is that any way to treat a tree?

(*Suddenly there is a scream and growling sounds. All animals start to shudder and shake. General ad libs: "Oh, it's WILMA!"; "Oh, my goodness, where are we?"; "What are we going to do?"; etc. They scatter for cover. WILMA comes through the house.*)

WILMA: Come on, Troll.

(*WILMA carries a large stick and rides in on the TROLL's back. TROLL is her servant, and is part animal and part man.*)

WILMA: Come on, Troll, you lazy thing. Always taking your time. If you don't hurry, I'm going to lock you in the pound for a month.

TROLL: I'm trying Mistress, I'm trying.

WILMA: (*Gets down off TROLL's back, and looks around.*) I've been looking for something to eat all day. I've got this craving for kid-ke-bob. Have you seen any wandering through the Zone lately?

TROLL: No, Mistress, I've been looking for weeks. They all must be happy at home these days. Haven't seen a teenager all month.

WILMA: Oh, I can't stand teenagers. They're too tough to eat. I like them young and tender. (*Acts as if she's eating them already, smacks lips.*) I've got to get some right away or I'll go out of my mind.

TROLL: Yes, Mistress, I'll try to help you find some.

WILMA: What do you mean "try"? You'd better get me some kids or I'll put you in the Torture Pound. Remember the last time? (*Starts toward him as if to begin the torture, and TROLL anxiously moves away.*)

TROLL: Oh, no, Mistress, please, please, I'll find you the kids ... please, I can't stand the torture, please, no ...

WILMA: (*Hits at him.*) Well, then you had better come up with something. I've got a strong feeling ... (*She sniffs.*) ... that there are some kids in the Zone and I want them, you understand?

TROLL: Yes, Mistress, I understand.

WILMA: I want them, because they taste so good. (*She licks her lips.*)

(*Song and Dance*)

KID-KE-BOB

Young and succulent, sweet and tender,
Better than frogs or fish,
Broiled, boiled or bar-be-qued,
Younguns are my favorite dish.

There ain't nothing like french-fried fingers
Or a french-fried pug nose,
And ooo-whee I sure do love
Snacking on plump pickled toes.

> Stuffed young cheeks make real good eats,
> They're hard to resist,
> But when it comes to gourmet treats
> Kid-ke-bob tops the list.

(*CHORUS*)
(Kid-ke-bob, kid-ke-bob bob)
Can chase away my gloom,
(Kid-ke-bob) I love it almost as much as
Riding on my broom./(*REPEAT*)

(*VAMP*)
Kid-ke-bob, Kid-ke-bob bob
Kid-ke-bob, Kid-ke-bob bob

(*Vamp through soft-shoe dance and end with chorus.*)

WILMA: Now get on with it, Troll. In the meantime, I'm going home and watch *Dallas*. J.R. is my main man.

(*She exits through the house humming the Song; TROLL moves about, scratching his head, acting very nervously.*)

TROLL: What am I going to do? I've got to find some kids. The Mistress will torture me if I don't. What am I going to do? ... I know, I know, I'll become invisible. I'll use this ca-ca potion

Mistress gave me. That way if there are kids about, no one will know I'm here.

(*TROLL swallows potion and behaves as if he is changing from Dr. Jeckyll into Mr. Hyde. He finally ends the struggle, stretched out on the floor.*)

TROLL: Oh, good grief, that was rough. (*He looks down at his body as he gets up.*) Great! It worked. I'm invisible. I'll just sit up here and watch. (*He sits on upstage area.*)

(*Suddenly, forest noises start and we see KIDS and ANIMALS approaching the area.*)

TREE: I think the coast is clear. Ole' Wilma was in rare form.

SARA: You can say that again. Look at me. I'm shaking all over.

CYNTHIA: Oh, be quiet, you're always shaking. You're a nervous wreck.

SARA: Well, what do you expect? What do you expect, I'm always having to look for nuts, look for nuts, nuts, nuts. What do you expect?

CLARABIRD: Here, have some bird seed. (*She pulls out a thermos.*) Oops, I mean bird juice. You'll feel better.

(*She starts to laugh. OWL NO. 2 joins her with laughter.*)

TREE: All right, that's enough of that. We've got to get Hansel and Gretel some place to stay so Wilma can't get them.

SARA: I know a place, I know a place.

CYNTHIA: You don't know anything.

SARA: Yes, I do, too; yes, I do, too; yes, I do, too.

CLARABIRD: Well, where for goodness sake? You're making me dizzy. Hiccup!

OWL NO. 2: Me too, me too!

SARA: In that cave; in that cave. (*She points to the cave behind TREE, in same area.*) I find lots of nuts there. It's really big, really big.

TREE: (*Looks behind her and sees cave.*) Well, will wonders never cease. I remember that cave from my youth. (*Laughs sexily*) At any rate, let's go kids, gather yourselves up and into the cave.

(*All the while TROLL is watching this, waiting for his chance. KIDS move into cave area.*)

Tree: Now remember, don't come out until we come for you.

Hansel and Gretel: Okay.

Hansel: When do we eat?

Gretel: Yeah, I'm kind of hungry.

Sara: I'll bring you some nuts, I'll bring you some nuts.

Cynthia: Oh, good grief, they need more than that.

Clarabird: What about some bird juice?

(She laughs. Owl No. 2 laughs with her.)

Owl No. 2: Bird juice. Bird juice.

Tree: Be quiet, all of you. Listen, kids. I'll bring you in some food as soon as it gets dark, okay?

Hansel and Gretel: Okay.

Tree: Now in you go.

(Children exit into cave. ALL ad lib: "See you later," etc.)

Tree: Gosh, I'm tired. Can't take all of this intrigue. I need my beauty sleep. (Stretches, yawns) Sing me a song, Mimic, a soothing one.

Owl No. 2:   Rock a bye baby
In a tree top
When the wind blows
The cradle will rock
When the bough breaks...

Tree: (Interrupts her, disturbed) Hold it a minute, can't have my limbs breaking. My shape is all I've got. Run along Mimic, you're depressing.

Owl No. 2: You're depressing...You're depressing. (Exits, giggling)

Tree: Think I'll just count sheep instead...One, two, three... huh, funny-looking little things...four, five, six...(She gets sleepier.)...seven, eight...

(She falls off to sleep. Troll has been watching all the while. Suddenly he perks up.)

Troll: I'll pour some knock-out drops over Tree here.

(Tree snores louder)

TROLL: Great. Now's my chance. Now I need to be visible again, I'll take the anti-caca potion. (*He swallows it. Same routine happens.*) Wow, that was rougher. Now, how do I get them out of the cave? I know, I'll pretend to be ole' Oakey here . . . let me see . . . (*Starts to talk and walk like her.*) . . . My shape's all I got. My shape's all I got. That's it. That's it. Now what do I tell the kids? I know, I'll tell them I've got food for them. (*Moves near cave area.*) Say, kids . . . yoo hoo, kids . . . Come on out, I've got some food for ya. Come on out!

(*HANSEL and GRETEL enter, rubbing eyes and looking tired.*)

GRETEL: Gosh, that was quick.

HANSEL: I'm really hungry.

(*Suddenly they see TROLL*)

HANSEL: Who are you? Where is Oakey?

GRETEL: Oh, Hansel, I don't like the way he looks. Hansel, I think he was with Wilma the Witch.

TROLL: (*Laughs*) That's right, I'm Troll, her servant, and you'll be coming with me.

HANSEL and GRETEL: (*They start to run.*) Oh, no, we're not.

TROLL: (*Runs after them.*) Oh, yes, you are.

(*They run through the house. There is a mad chase with screaming, etc. Finally he catches them.*)

TROLL: I've got you. I've got you.

(*He takes his rope from his waist and ties and gags them. GRETEL bites his fingers.*)

TROLL: Why, you little brat. (*He continues to tie them up, laughing all the while.*) Mistress, Mistress, kid-ke-bob, kid-ke-bob. (*TROLL takes KIDS off.*)

END OF ACT ONE

Act Two

(*IRMA and FLORENCE enter the livingroom. HERMAN is still asleep on the couch.*)

FLORENCE: Wait a minute, I think I saw him move his arm.

IRMA: Well, let's try the spell again.

(*They begin the ritual with tambourines. SAM THE FROG and PEARLIE THE OWL enter from outside the house.*)

FROG: Okay, when I get into the house, you scream. (*He enters the house through the back way, or window.*)

OWL No. 1: (*Screams and enters house through the back way.*)

(*We hear IRMA and FLORENCE really dancing in great gypsy style—tambourines, etc. Suddenly, there is a loud scream from OWL No. 1. IRMA and FLORENCE stop suddenly.*)

FLORENCE: My goodness, what was that!

IRMA: I don't know. It came from outside.

(*They peer out the window. While they're looking out, OWL No. 1 and FROG sneak into the house with large mallets.*)

FLORENCE: I don't see anything, do you?

IRMA: No, but it sounded like it came from across the yard. We've been having a lot of trouble with burglars lately.

FLORENCE: Oh, darling, don't remind me. I get so frightened just thinking about them . . .

(*Before she ends the sentence, OWL No. 1 and FROG hit them over the head and they fall down.*)

FROG: Great. Now let's use the magic sleepwalking spell to get them out of here.

OWL No. 1: That's a good idea.

FROG: Do you remember the words?

OWL NO. 1: Yeah. Are you ready?

FROG: Ready.

FROG and OWL NO. 1: (*Voodoo ritual*)

> Amity, Amity, Amity
> These women are causing a calamity
> Eyes closed, arms out . . .
> Move that 'a way, that 'a way
>
> Hocus pocus
> Keep in focus
> Down the hall
> Into the closet
>
> Lock yourself in
> Stand there and grin
> Hocus pocus
> Keep in focus.

FROG: Great. Now let's get the anti-potion into Herman. If we press these two nerves on his neck, his mouth will open.

(*They pour the potion into HERMAN's mouth, holding his head up to do so. Suddenly, HERMAN awakens and straightens himself up, looking around in a daze.*)

HERMAN: What's going on? Where am I? Who are you? What are you doing here?

FROG: Now just take it easy, Herm ole' boy. We're just here to help you.

OWL NO. 1: You see, you've been under a spell.

HERMAN: What do you mean "spell"? I'm fine. Where's Irma?

FROG: Do you remember anything at all?

HERMAN: Well, I remember coming home from work . . . Oh, oh, yes, Irma and Florence were here and I had some tea with them.

OWL NO. 1: Did you see *them* drink it?

HERMAN: Well, no, as a matter of fact, I didn't. You see, I've been under a strain. I was so tired.

FROG: Listen, Herman, we're trying to help you. This may come as a shock to you but Irma and Florence drugged you and then they put you under a spell.

OWL NO. 1: At least they were trying to.

HERMAN: I don't understand.

FROG: Well, it's like this. Ole' Irma wants you to send the kids off to a foster home so that she doesn't have to spend any extra money on them until you get a job.

HERMAN: I don't believe that.

FROG and OWL No. 1: It's the truth. Honest.

HERMAN: But we have extra money in the bank.

FROG: I'm afraid that's all been spent. She bought clothes and a fur coat and other things with that.

HERMAN: I don't know what to say. This is so unbelievable. Where is Irma? I want to talk to her right now.

FROG: Don't worry, Herman. We took care of her and her companion, Florence.

HERMAN: I can't believe any of this. I wouldn't send my children away.

NO WAY

No way would I ever send my angels
off to stay with strangers,
Although last September I gave in and
let them go with the Junior Rangers,
That was just for overnight—
Nothing more than overnight.

No, sir, there's no way that I'll be giving
in to her, not this time,
Before she could twist me 'round her finger
but no more, you can bet in this I'm
Burning up and hopping mad,
They're my kids and I'm their dad
And I want to know there's a roof overhead
And their stomachs are fed
When they're tucked into bed,
For wherever I am,
Rich or poor as I am,
For my Hansel and Gretel it's home.

They should be home now. Where are they, anyway?

OWL No. 1: We sent them to the Twilight Zone to be taken care of until we straighten out your head.

FROG: There's only one problem with it. Wilma the Witch is there and she hates kids, but loves how they taste. So we've got to get Hansel and Gretel out soon.

OWL NO. 1: Yeah, we haven't been able to get rid of Wilma and her torture stick. She was flying over the Zone one day going to a witch hunt and her broom broke. She's been with us ever since.

HERMAN: Well, we'd better get going. How do we get there? Where is it? Where is this Twilight Zone?

FROG: Well, it's kind of hard to explain.

OWL NO. 1: It's never, never land. It's Imagination Station, it's Dreamland, it's the Friendly Skies, it's everyplace you'd ever want to go.

THE TWILIGHT ZONE

Turn your eyes inside out
And search the back of your mind
There in a corner in a soft gray light you'll find
What's known as the Twilight Zone.

It's a place where nothing's black or white
It's always maybe or might,
And you're always just on the verge of things
That are almost but not quite.

And 'though things that you see appear to be real
They're never as real as they seem
It's a little like being half asleep
You're almost, but not quite, in a dream.

So turn your eyes outside in
And search the back of your mind
There in a corner in a soft gray light
You'll find what's known
As the Twilight Zone.

Come along (come along) to the Twilight Zone,
"   "   "   "   "   "   "   "   "
"   "   "   "   "   "   "   "   " .

(Continue to fade-out)

FROG: (As the song ends) Let's go out the back way. We'll get to the Zone faster.

(They exit. Lights fade up on Forest Area. TREE is still snoring. SARA THE SQUIRREL and CYNTHIA THE COCKATOO enter the forest, arguing.)

CYNTHIA: I told you already, nobody wants to eat nuts all the time. They scramble your brains; look at you, how you act.

SARA: Nuts are good for you, good for you. They're so crunchy and munchy, yes, that's right, crunchy and munchy. I love 'em because they're crunchy and munchy ... crunchy ...

CYNTHIA: Oh, shut up. You drive me to drink. Where's Clarabird?

(*Looks around for* CLARABIRD *while* SARA *is counting nuts and repeating "crunchy and munchy" to herself. She calls for* CLARABIRD.)

CYNTHIA: Clara ... Clara ... Clara ... Clarabird ...

CLARABIRD: (*Enters, flying somewhat zigzagedly.*) Hi guys, fly the friendly skies, guys. Happy new year! Happy new year! Happy new year!

CYNTHIA: Slow down, slow down a minute. Do you have any sherry? Sara has wrecked my last nerve.

SARA: (*Still counting nuts.*) Crunchy, munchy ...

CYNTHIA: See what I mean? If she keeps this up, I'm going to have to put her back in the Home!

CLARABIRD: Wow! The Home! Oh, it's murder there ... no place for a fun-loving person. (*She hiccups.*)

CYNTHIA: Well, do you have any or not?

CLARABIRD: Any what?

CYNTHIA: Oh, I don't believe this. Any sherry. My nerves, remember?

CLARABIRD: Oh, oh yes. I don't have any with me. Tree took my last bottle. Let's go over and get it from her; maybe she has some left. (*She hiccups.*) Come on. (*She leads the way. Suddenly she bumps into* TREE.) Holy Moses. Tree, wake up. I gotta talk to you. (TREE *remains asleep.*) Hey, Tree ... Oakey ... Oakey Tree, wake up. (*She shakes her.*) Boy, man o'man, what did she have to drink?

(CYNTHIA *and* SARA *try to wake her up.*)

CYNTHIA: Say, something must be wrong with her.

SARA: (*Scared*) Oh, no, oh, no, not Oakey, not Oakey, I'll give her some nuts, I'll give her some nuts. That should do it, that should do it.

CYNTHIA: Should do what! Will you calm down? Maybe Hansel and Gretel know what happened. Sara, get them from the cave.

(*Meanwhile,* CYNTHIA *and* CLARABIRD *continue to try to wake* TREE.

SARA goes to the cave and immediately returns, screaming and jumping up and down.)

SARA: They're gone. They're gone. They're gone. They're gone.

CYNTHIA: What do you mean *gone*? Where could they go? I don't believe you. *(She goes to the cave and looks in.. She returns immediately.)* Oh, no. They're gone.

SARA: I told you, I told you, I told you.

CYNTHIA: Yeah, okay, okay. You told me.

CLARABIRD: Oh dear, this ain't no happy new year. I betcha Wilma's got them.

CYNTHIA: What makes you think that?

CLARABIRD: Oakey here was guarding the cave—we can't wake her up—betcha she got ole' Troll's sleeping powder in her trunk.

CYNTHIA: We'd better get some help because if Wilma gets her habits on, those kids are goners.

SARA: Oh, my goodness, oh, my goodness.

(FROG, HERMAN, and OWL NO.1 appear.)

FROG: So here you are. We've been looking everywhere for you.

OWL NO. 1: Where's Mimic and where are Hansel and Gretel?

(All ANIMALS say nothing.)

OWL NO. 1: I said, where's Hansel and Gretel?

(Still no answer. Suddenly they all act like animals, using animal sounds.)

FROG: Okay, okay, I get it. It's all right. Herman, here, is Hansel and Gretel's father. He's not here to hurt you. So, please, now tell us where the kids are.

HERMAN: Yes, please, I've got to find them and take them home.

(All ANIMALS start to talk at once.)

ALL: Well, you see, we think Wilma's got them ...

OWL NO. 1: What! You're kidding me. Where's Mimic? I told that crazy bird to look after them. What're we're gonna do?

(Suddenly OWL NO. 2 comes running in, screaming.)

OWL NO. 2: Help. Help. Oh, my good grief, help, help.

(*OWL NO. 1 and FROG slow her down.*)

FROG: Hold on now, Mimic, what's wrong?

OWL NO. 2: I saw them, I saw them.

OWL NO. 1: You saw who?

OWL NO. 2: I saw Wilma. She's got the kids. She's tied them up and is getting ready to . . . to . . .

OWL NO. 1: To what?

OWL NO. 2: You know . . . you know . . . she's got her salad, french fries, and a cold beer, and now she's gonna . . . gonna . . .

OWL NO. 1: Oh, no . . . kid-ke-bob!

(*CLARABIRD swoons and faints. CYNTHIA screams. SARA tries to calm CYNTHIA.*)

SARA: Oh, no, my goodness, oh, no, my goodness.

HERMAN: Well, which way do we go? We've got to save them.

OWL NO. 2: It's that-a-way.

(*They all start to run toward the house.*)

OWL NO. 2: Wait. No, it's that-a-way.

(*They all start toward stage right.*)

OWL NO. 2: Wait. No, it's that-a-way.

(*They go the other way. During these movements, the* William Tell Overture *is heard and stopped each time they stop.*)

CLARABIRD: Wait a minute. I can't take much more of this. I'm starting to feel sick.

FROG: Oh, no you don't . . . not now. We need all the help we can get because Wilma the Witch and Troll the Mold can eat kids alive and that ain't no jive. Pearlie, throw some of the anti-potion on Oakey so she'll wake up.

(*OWL NO. 1 throws potion on TREE.*)

FROG: Okay, everybody, something tells me it's this-a-way. (*Exits through the house.*)

TREE: (*Slowly wakes up.*) Boy, what a dream. Treetop is such a gorgeous guy. (*Tries to walk.*) My goodness, feel like I've been doped up. It's this clean air, sometimes it gets the best of me. (*Stretches*) A little pollution never hurt anyone. I'd better feed the

TREE (con't.)

kids. I wonder if the Burger Queen is still open. (*Starts toward the cave.*) Hey, kids, kids, come on out, you must be starving. Sorry I overslept. Hey, kids ... kids ... (*Realizing they're not there.*) Oh, no, where are they? (*Starts to rush around looking and is very unsteady on her feet.*) Good grief, what's the matter with me? My legs feel wobbly. The last time that happened ole' Troll the Mold slipped a sleeping potion in my soda. Oh ... oh, that's it. Wilma's got the kids.

(*Suddenly there are shrieks of laughter from WILMA and TROLL as they enter through the house with the kids tied up. TROLL is carrying a tray with salad, french fries, and beer for WILMA.*)

TREE: Oh, no, it's Wilma. (*She pretends to be doped.*)

WILMA: Come on, Troll, I feel like having a picnic. Put the kids under that tree there.

(*HANSEL and GRETEL lean against TREE, who signals them to keep quiet.*)

WILMA: Hurry up, Troll. I'm starving to death. Two hours without food is enough to kill you.

TROLL: Yes, Mistress, I'm coming, I'm coming.

(*WILMA places blanket downstage of TREE and begins unloading the picnic basket.*)

WILMA: No-frills beer. Reaganomics will never get the best of me. Let's see now, I need to toast my sesame seed buns and get the skewers ready.

(*She takes out giant pieces of bread and very large skewers, which frighten the KIDS. TROLL is helping set up the area. TREE unties the KIDS without WILMA and TROLL noticing. She continues to pretend she's sleeping.*)

GRETEL: Oh, Hansel, I'm scared. What's going to happen?

HANSEL: Don't worry, Gretel, I'll think of something.

WILMA: Shut up over there. Don't waste your time talking, you'll lose too much energy and then ruin your flavor. So cool it, you understand?

(*TROLL laughs. WILMA looks at him and he suddenly stops laughing. WILMA and TROLL continue to set up the area. TREE whispers to HANSEL about what he should do while WILMA continues to set up.*)

HANSEL: (*Whispering*) Gretel, I've got an idea. Why don't you start crying real loud and when she screams at you, pretend to faint?

GRETEL: What good will that do?

HANSEL: Just do it, you'll see.

(GRETEL *begins to cry loudly.*)
WILMA: I say shut up. You're losing your flavor, you little brat.

(GRETEL *crys louder.*)
WILMA: Okay if that's the way you want it. Troll, get me my stick.

(TROLL *gets the stick;* WILMA *moves toward* GRETEL *and threatens her.* GRETEL *faints.*)
WILMA: Wake up, you little brat, wake up. What's the matter with you? (WILMA *shakes and pokes* GRETEL.)

HANSEL: She often faints like that. She's anemic.

WILMA: Anemic, anemic—Troll, what is anemic?

(TREE *begins to untie* HANSEL *and* GRETEL.)
TROLL: That means she doesn't have enough blood.

WILMA: (*Screams*) What! You don't mean . . . you can't mean . . . she's a . . . a vampire.

TROLL: (*Shakes head to say yes.*) Yes, Mistress.

WILMA: (*Getting hysterical*) Oh, no, I can't stand it. I hate vamps. They're really tasteless. Oh, I can't stand it.

TROLL: But Mistress, you still have the boy.

WILMA: (*Calming down*) Yeah, you're right. I still have the boy.

(*She turns to get him.* HANSEL *and* GRETEL *start to attack and run, along with* TREE.)
HANSEL: Oh, no, you don't. Get back, you old witch, you.

TREE: Run, kids. I'll do the blocking. I was a great football player.

HANSEL: Come on, Gretel, run.

(*There is a mad chase. Suddenly all the* ANIMALS *and* HERMAN *appear. The chase—to the* William Tell Overture—*continues until the* WITCH *and* TROLL *are captured and tied by* FROG *and* OWL NO. 1. *Ad libs are heard during the chase.*)
SARA: Get um, get um, get um

CYNTHIA: Beat the witch
            Beat the witch
            Beat the witch

CLARABIRD: Juice her, juice her

OWL NO. 2: Ride um cowboy
            Ride um cowboy

FROG: Finally. Okay, Wilma, this is it.

OWL NO. 1: Yeah, we've had it with your craziness.

OWL NO. 2: Craziness, craziness.

WILMA: Say, look, you guys, I was only kidding.

HANSEL: No she wasn't. She was going to eat us alive.

GRETEL: And that ain't no jive.

HERMAN: Don't worry, kids. I'm here to protect you.

ANIMALS: We're all here to protect you from all evil. Truth, justice and the Ukranian way. (ANIMALS salute and click heels.)

WILMA: What do you mean "evil"? I'm not evil.

TROLL: Mistress, you don't mean that.

WILMA: Shut up, Troll, I'm, trying to sham these suckers. Say, look, everybody, I'm just out to have a little fun. Every morning I take a run and have some fun. You know what I mean? Now come on, cut me loose, you silly goose.

FROG: (To the ANIMALS) What do you think, guys?

OWL NO. 1: Sam, are you crazy? You know she doesn't mean all that.

FROG: Well, people can change.

OWL NO. 1: Not Wilma, she has a record of felonies, misdemeanors, larceny, etc., etc., etc.

FROG: Well, what are we going to do with her?

ANIMALS: Send her back to Ca-Ca Land.
          Send her back to Ca-Ca Land.
          Send her back to Ca-Ca Land.
          Send her back to Ca-Ca Land.

(Note: Above action done in cheerleading fashion.)

FROG: But how? She broke her broom, remember?

HERMAN: Broom? Did you say broom? Look, I can fix it; that was part of my job at the plant. I designed and built brooms and vacuum cleaners. Where is it?

FROG: Okay, Herman, you got a deal. The broom's in the cave. Get it, kids. Maybe the Zone will get back to normal without Wilma around.

SARA: Yeah, we need to be normal again, normal again . . .

CYNTHIA: Normal for you is nuts.

SARA: Nuts, they're crunchy and munchy, crunchy and munchy . . .

CYNTHIA: Oh, good grief, not again.

CLARABIRD: Have a drink. (*There is nothing left in the thermos.*) Well, I tried. Happy new year.

TREE: This is normal?

OWL NO. 2: This is normal? (*Laughs*) Have a drink. Crunchy and munchy.

HERMAN: All right, if I am going to fix the broom, I need glue, tape, and feathers.

CLARABIRD: I have the glue.

SARA: I have some tape.

CYNTHIA: You can have some of my feathers.

(*Disco music begins*)
(*ANIMALS circle HERMAN, HANSEL and GRETEL, FROG, and OWL NO. 1, and ad lib with "He's a genius," "Look how clever," "My, my, a wonder," etc.*)
HERMAN: Okay. There, it's finished.

(*All applaud*)
FROG: (*Crosses to WILMA and TROLL.*) Okay, Wilma, the jig is up.

ALL: The jig is up.

WILMA: "Jig"? You sure are corny.

FROG: Untie them kids.

(*They do.*)

FROG: Okay, here's your broom. Take off.

WILMA: Give me a chance, I'll take you off . . . all of ya.

(CROWD jeers: Boo-jeer, Boo-jeer, Boo-jeer.)
WILMA: Okay, okay, I can tell when I'm not wanted. Come on, Troll, let's beat it. This place is boring, anyway. Come on, Troll, get the broom.

TROLL: Yes, Mistress, yes.

(He gets on the broom and WILMA gets on his back.)
WILMA: Dumb place, poor accommodations, nuts to this place.

SARA: Nuts. They're crunchy and munchy.

ALL: SHUT UP!!!

WILMA: Are you ready, Troll?

TROLL: Yes, Mistress, yes.

WILMA: Well, let's go, you old mold.

(They take off.)
WILMA: Wheeee! Broom riding is a gas.

TROLL: Yes, Mistress, yes. Wheeee!

(They exit.)
HANSEL and GRETEL: And your mother rides a vacuum cleaner.

HERMAN: Well, children, shall we go home?

GRETEL: Oh. boy, am I ever ready to go home.

HANSEL: Wait a minute, what about Irma?

HERMAN: Oh, don't worry about her. As soon as I get home, I will send her on her way. After all, we're about love, us three, right?

HANSEL and GRETEL: Right.

HERMAN: (To ANIMALS) Oh, which way do we go?

SARA: (Pointing to the right) That-a-way.

CYNTHIA: (Pointing to the left) No, no, this-a-way.

CLARABIRD: (Pointing straight up) No, that-a-way.

OWL NO. 2: (*Laughs, points up*) No, that-a-way.

OWL NO. 1: You shut up.

TREE: You can say that to all of them. I'm getting seasick. Now, hold on, everybody. Will somebody please tell me how do they get home?

FROG: Oh, it's very simple—you guys really ought to remember this. Just click your heels three times . . .

OWL NO. 1: Uh, Sam, that's another play.

FROG: Oh, sorry 'bout that. Home . . . where is home?

OWL NO. 1: It's where your heart is.

FROG: Or better still, it's where your head is.

HANSEL: Well, our heart and head is with our friends, right, Gretel?

GRETEL: Right, Hansel.

HANSEL and GRETEL: Right, Father?

HERMAN: Right! I want to thank all of you for helping to take care of my children.

FROG: Well, what are friends for if we can't help?

OWL NO. 1: Yeah, what are friends for?

ALL: We know!

FRIENDSHIP

A Friend	Is there in a pinch
"	Never runs from trouble
"	When you're in a fix
"	Is there on the double
"	Will not let you down
"	When you're in a pickle
"	If he's got a dime
"	You've got a nickel.
	Friendship, friendship
	There's no better ship than friendship.
A Friend	Is there when it rains
"	Not just when it's sunny
"	Will laugh at your jokes

"	Even though they're not funny,
"	Is there when you lose
"	Not only when you're winning
"	When you're all tied up
"	Will go an extra inning.
	Friendship, friendship
	There's no better ship than friendship

There are tall ships and small ships
And scholarships and fellowships
And every other kind of ship—but
Friendship, friendship
There's no better ship than
(Modulate) Friendship, friendship
There's no better ship than friendship

(At the end of FRIENDSHIP, forest music comes in. ANIMALS repeat opening scene of building forest. HANSEL and GRETEL begin exit for home.)

HERMAN: You know, children, I think it's this way.

(They move upstage through the cave and enter the house.)

(ANIMALS freeze.)

(MUSIC OUT)

HANSEL and GRETEL: Hooray, we're home.

GRETEL: Oh, Father, I'm so happy.

HANSEL: Me, too.

HERMAN and ANIMALS: *(Sing)*

NO WAY TAG

For wherever I am
Rich or poor as I am
For my Hansel and Gretel
It's home.

HANSEL and GRETEL: We love you, Father.

HERMAN: And I love you, too.

ANIMALS: *(Repeating to each other)* I love you, I love you, I love you.

Music fades out

END OF PLAY

PROPS:

Nail file
Masking tape
Glue
Feathers
Whistle
Scrub brushes (2)
Cups and saucers (3)
Tray
Paper with "magic" words written on it
Buckets (2)
Set of schoolbooks (2)
Tambourines (2)
Lunch bags (2)
Large stack of newspapers
Bottle containing "potion"
Mallet made of foam
Broom (for Witch)
Broken stick, witch's broom, hidden in cave
Picnic basket
Sesame seed buns made of foam
Six-pack of "no-frills" beer
Skewers
Rope (to tie up Hansel and Gretel)

COSTUME SUGGESTIONS:

SAM THE FROG: Green sweatshirt or tunic top, belted at the waist, with bow tie and green turtleneck worn under tunic. Green jeans or green tights and soft shoes.

IRMA: Lounging dress or pajamas. Gypsy costume could be a loud-colored skirt and off-the-shoulder blouse in contrasting color, lots of bracelets, and dangling earrings.

HERMAN: Dark business suit, white shirt, tie, and hat.

HANSEL: Coveralls or jeans, checkered shirt or t-shirt, baseball cap worn sideways, and jacket for school.

GRETEL: Skirt and blouse covered with patches, knee socks, jacket for school.

PEARLIE THE OWL NO. 1: Graduation robe and cap, large, rounded glasses. (Robe should be a bright color, yellow or red.)

MIMIC THE OWL NO. 2: Knee-length tunic in same color as PEARLIE. Undergarment could be leotard top, or sleeves in tunic could be made of some mesh material. Argyle socks. Headpiece could be feathers attached to a bathing cap.

OAKEY THE TREE: A long gown with ruffled collar and sleeves; skirt split up the center á la Carmen Miranda. Head gear could be pillbox cap covered in dress material using wire or pipe cleaners to attach branchlike antennae to hat.

SARA THE SQUIRREL: Leotards and tights worn under a romper-like body suit with a bright scarf around the neck. A fur hat with squirrel ears attached. A bag hung around the neck for the storing of nuts.

CYNTHIA THE COCKATOO: Harem pants and top in bright colors with long feathers attached to skullcap.

WILMA THE WITCH: Red knickers with red blouse top, black boots, a black wide-brim hat with a red flower attached, and a black cape.

TROLL THE MOLD: Dark brown or rust tunic and ragged pants, karate style, both with ragged edges. A pouch to carry ca-ca potion. Facial make-up should look as though he was covered with mud.

SET DESIGN:

Proscenium or Thrust: The house should be upstage, elevated on several platforms, with exit to the remainder of the house stage right, entrance into the house stage left. The window is mimed downstage center. Stage right furniture includes couch center stage, coffee table, easy chair downstage left, endtable at stage right of couch for the telephone, and bookcase upstage left where books, potion, and words for magic spell are stored.

Downstage area should be used as the forest area. Downstage right should be a well or rocklike structure for FROG's house. Downstage left should be a cave. Slightly down of cave should be another rocklike structure.

Note for the Twilight Zone Sequence:

Decorative eye masks should be used by the forest creatures, as well as strobe lights. If strobe lights are not available, confetti and streamers can be used to establish the Twilight Zone, along with rock music and gymnastic movements, cartwheels, etc.

MUSIC APPENDIX

CROESUS AND THE WITCH
- Overture
- Story Telling Time
- You Can Do What You Wanna Do
- Out There in the Forest
- Forest Dance
- Horrible Hecuba
- If I Had a Horseshoe (Mathew)
- They Were Warned
- If I Had a Horseshoe (Ephram)
- They Were Warned (Reprise)
- If I Had a Horseshoe (Croesus)
- AHA
- So High, So Wide, So Deep
- So Long, So Wide (Dance)
- So High (Exit Music)
- They Were Warned (Reprise)
- If I Had a Horseshoe (Reprise)
- You Can Do What You Wanna Do (Reprise)
- AHA (Reprise)
- Throwing Stones
- Finale

HANSEL AND GRETEL
- Good Old Irma
- Children Need Discipline
- Friendship
- Tree's Lament
- Kid-Ke-Bob
- No Way
- The Twilight Zone
- The Twilight Zone (Dance)

OVERTURE

ALLEGRO, MM= 𝅗𝅥=120

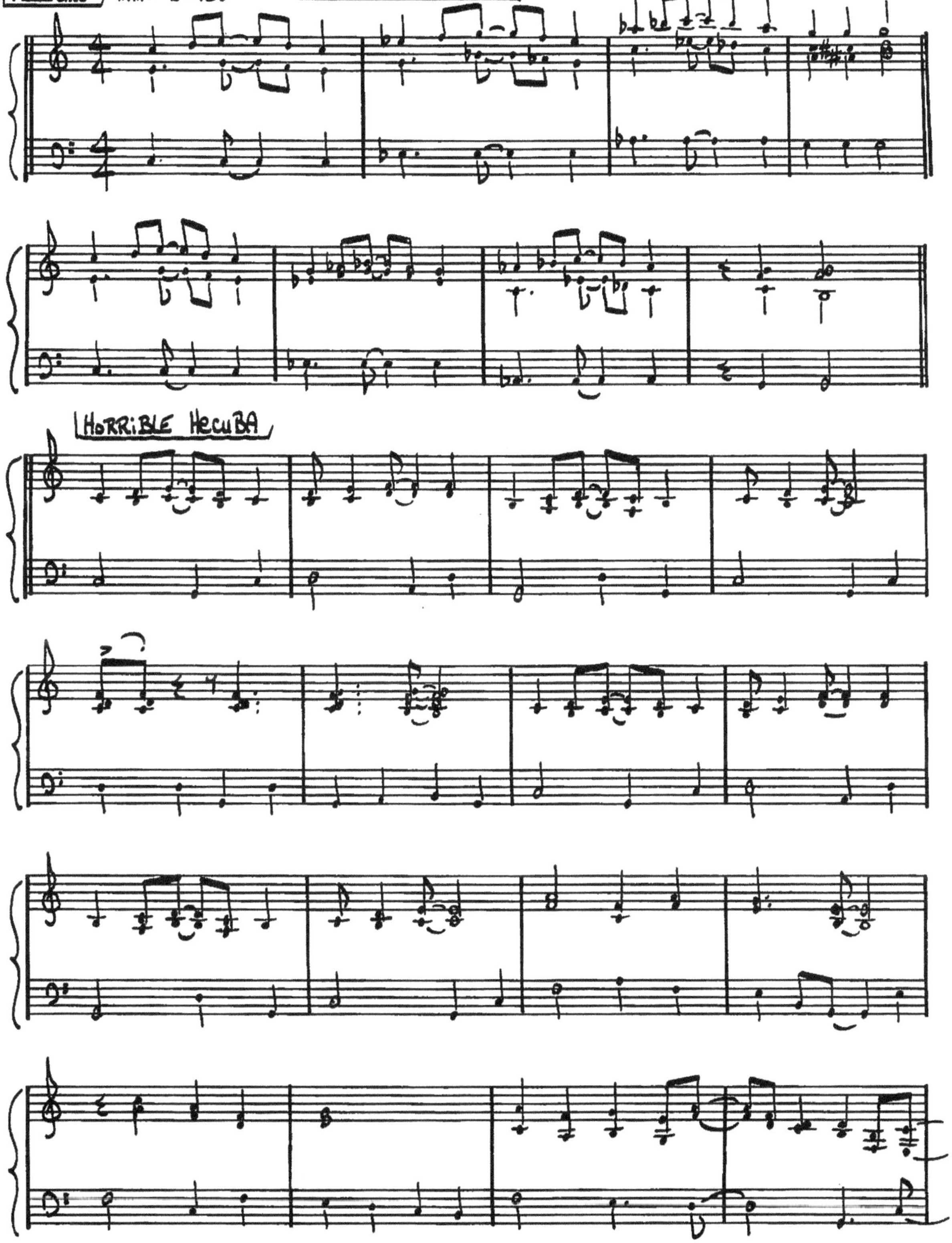

OUT THERE IN THE FOREST

MM ♩ = 112

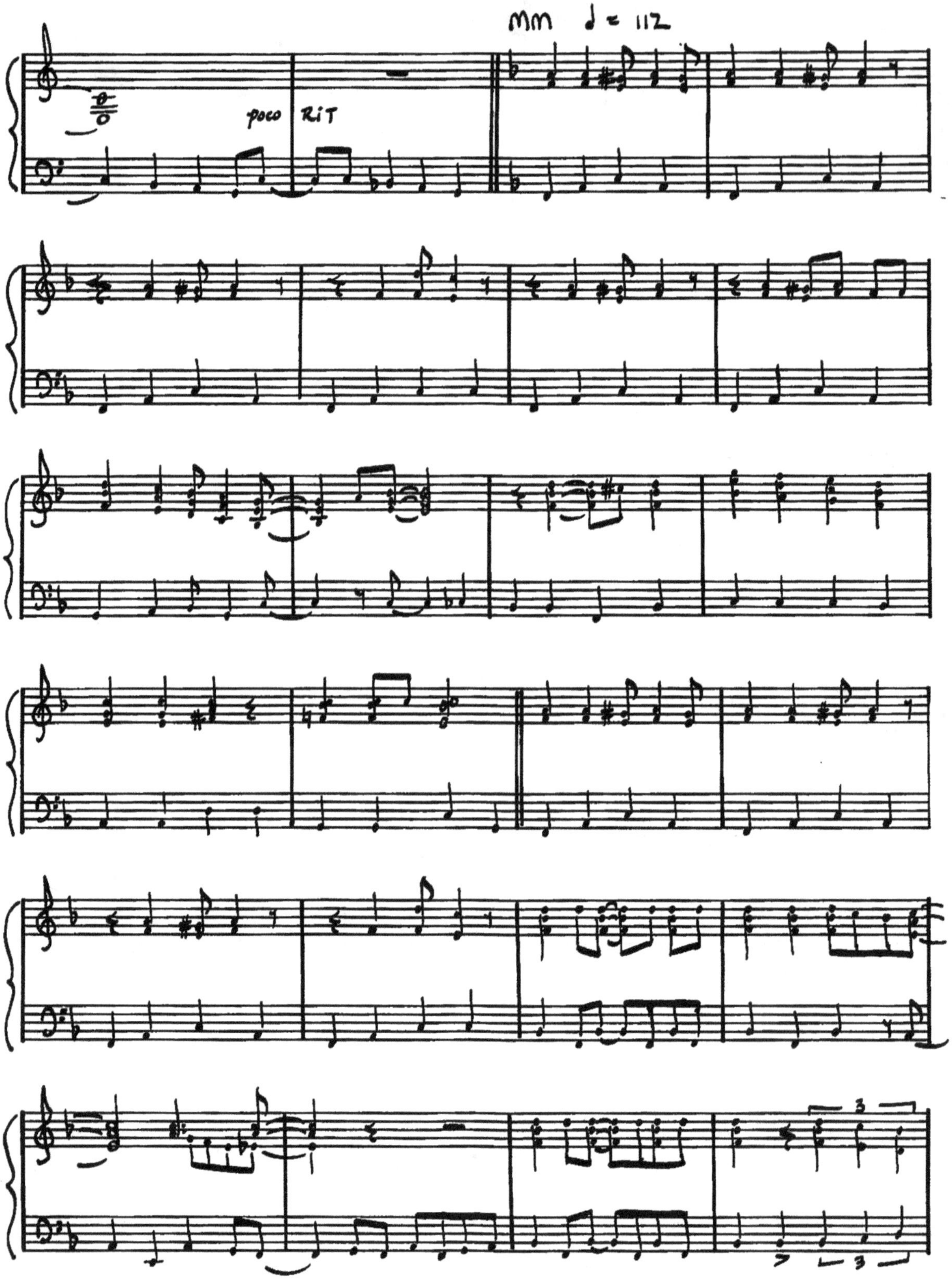

Story Telling Time mm ♩ = 72

Story Telling Time

mm ♩= 72

(Verse 1)
STOR - Y TELL-ing Time is HERE ___ STOR-Y TELL-ing Time ___

(Verse 2)
STOR - Y. TELL-ing Time is HERE ___ STOR-Y TELL-ing Time ___

WAN-NA TAKE You SOME-PLACE THAT You've NEV-ER BEEN ___ WE'LL

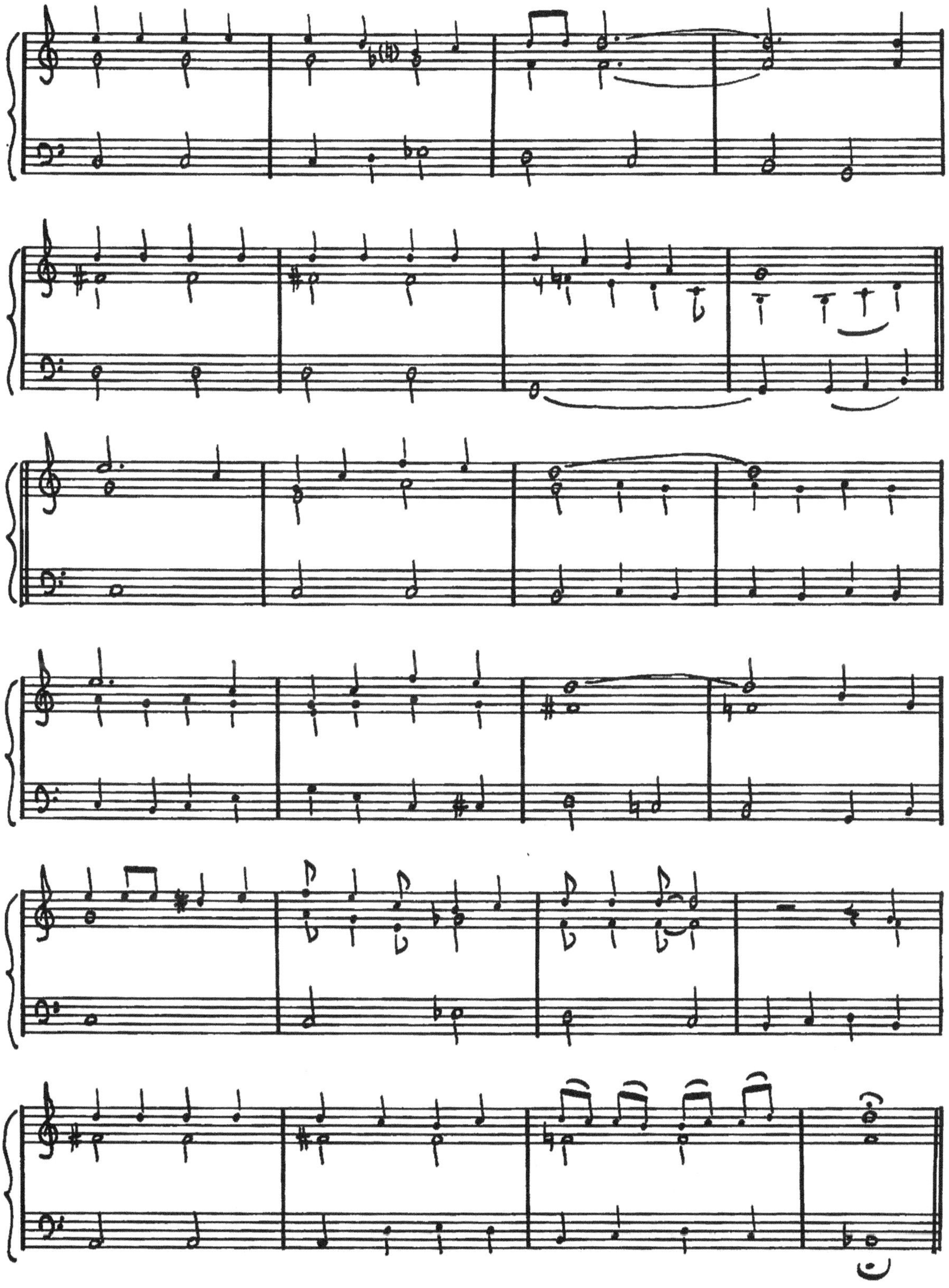

TAKE YOU TO AN- OTH-ER PLACE _ AND BRING YOU BACK A-GAIN ___

STOR- Y TELL-ING TIME _ IS HERE ___ STOR-Y TELL-ING TIME ___

STOR- Y TELL-ING TIME _ IS HERE ___ STOR-Y TELL-ING TIME ___

USE YOUR I- MA-GI- NA- TION AND IT WILL BE A TREAT ___ BUT

FIRST I HAVE SOME FRIENDS THAT I WOULD LIKE FOR YOU TO MEET   I AM

mm ♩ = 96

(NAME ____) I AM (NAME ____) I AM (NAME ____) I AM (NAME ____) I AM

(NAME ____)   I AM (NAME ____) AND THEY PLAY __ WHAT DO YOU PLAY?

Rit.

A TEMPO

WAT-ER DEER A-CORNS FOR-ESTS CORN MOUN-TAINS AND MAN-Y MAN-Y

MAN-Y MAN-Y MAN-Y MAN-Y MAN-Y MAN-Y MAN-Y MAN-Y MAN-Y MAN-Y MAN-Y MAN-Y MAN-Y MAN-Y MAN-Y MAN-Y ALL RIGHT

[A TEMPO]

OTH-ERS   I AM (NAME _____) AND I PLAY MATH-ew   I AM

(NAME _____) AND I PLAY E-PHRAM   I AM   (NAME ____) AND I PLAY

CROE-SUS   AND I AM (NAME ____) AND I PLAY GUESS WHO

MM 𝅗𝅥 = 72
STOR- Y TELL-ING TIME IS HERE
STOR-Y TELL-ING TIME
STOR- Y TELL-ING TIME IS HERE
STOR-Y TELL-ING TIME
WAN-NA TAKE YOU SOME PLACE THAT YOU'VE NEV-ER BEEN
WE'LL
TAKE YOU TO AN- OTH ER TIME AND BRING YOU BACK A- GAIN

STOR- Y TELL-ING TIME IS HERE ___ STOR-Y TELL-ING TIME ___

STOR- Y TELL-ING TIME IS HERE ___ STOR-Y TELL-ING TIME ___

STOR- Y TELL-ING TIME ___ IS

HERE ___

You Can Do What You Wanna Do

ALLEGRO
MM ♩=132
[MOD. ROCK]

NO USE SIT-TING WAIT-ING FOR SOME-THING TO HAP-

PEN _____ SIT-TING TWID-DLING YOUR

FIN-GERS AND YOUR TOES _____

You Can Be out MAK-ING Your own THING HAP-PEN

IN-STEAD OF SIT-TING HOME SCRATCH-ING YOUR NOSE

CHORUS

You CAN GET WHAT YOU WAN-NA GET

You CAN GO WHERE YOU WAN-NA GO   You CAN

DO WHAT YOU WAN-NA DO___ BY_ DO-ING IT
TO- DAY WILL BE YES- TER-DAY___ TO-
MOR- ROW___ IF YOU WANT TO SIT_
_ A- ROUND_ AND WAIT___

You will just be hun-gri-er to-mor-row

and you won't have an-y grits to put on your plate

You can get what you wan-na get

You can go where you wan-na go You can

Do what you wan-na Do _____ BY _ Do-ing it

You Can   Get Where You wan-na Get _____   You Can

Go Where You wan-na Go _____   You Can   Do What You wan-na Do _____

_   BY Do-ing it   BY

Do-ing it — BY Do-ing it

Out There In The Forest

Fast 4   mm ♩ = 168

our pock-ets — are emp-ty — our cup-boards — are bare —

the win-ter — is com-ing and we've got no win-ter clothes — to wear —

ALL _ OF OUR NEIGH-BORS ARE AS POOR AS CHURCH MICE TOO HERE'S WHAT WE'LL DO

WE'LL GO HUNT-ING AND KILL SOME DEER_ ON-LY AS MUCH AND NO MORE THAN WE NEED_

ev' RY one_will HAVE A DEER-SKIN JACK-ET TO WEAR _____

ev' RY one_will HAVE SWEET DEER_MEAT TO EAT

OUT THERE IN THE FOR- EST THERE ARE PLEN-TY OF DEER __ ROAM-ING A-ROUND __

OUT THERE IN THE FOR- EST WE CAN GET WHAT WE NEED __ TO FEED THE PEO-PLE

AL CODA

GET WHAT WE NEED __ TO FEED THE PEO-PLE GET WHAT WE NEED __ TO

Rit

FEED THE PEO-PLE GET WHAT WE NEED TO FEED THE PEO-PLE __

FOREST DANCE

V.S.

Lyrics:
GOT WHAT WE NEED TO FEED THE PEO-PLE GOT WHAT WE NEED TO FEED THE PEO-PLE GOT WHAT WE NEED TO FEED THE PEO-PLE

ev-RY-ONE __ WILL HAVE A DEER-SKIN JACK-ET TO WEAR __

ev'-ry one_ will have sweet DEER_ MEAT to

EAT

out there in the FOR-

est there are PLENT-Y of DEER_ ROAM-ing A-ROUND_

out there in the FOR- est we can get what we need_ To

FEED THE PEO-PLE GET WHAT WE NEED TO FEED THE PEO-PLE

GET WHAT WE NEED TO FEED THE

PEO-PLE

HORRIBLE HECUBA

mm ♩=160

Hec-u-BA___ A MEAN OLD WITCH_ WITH A HEART OF STONE_ AND A

BAG OF TRICKS_ TO TRICK YA_____

SHE'LL PRE-TEND_ TO BE NICE AS PIE_ BUT IF YOU LOOK_ IN HER

E-VIL EYE_ SHE'LL FIX YA_____ SO

HUN-TERS _ TAKE CARE BE- WARE OF

HEART-LESS HATE-FUL HOR- RI-BLE HE-CU-BA _

SHE LIVES DOWN _ IN A DEEP DARK DITCH_ WITH THE STO: -LEN GOODS_ THAT HAVE

MADE HER RICH _ AND GREED-Y _ SHE

ROBS THE WEALTH- Y AND FUR- THER MORE___ SHE WILL EV- EN

ROB THE POOR___ AND NEED- Y___ SO

HUN- TERS ___ TAKE CARE BE- WARE OF

HEART-LESS HATE-FUL HOR- RI-BLE HE-CU-BA___

You BET-TER TAKE CARE AND BE - WARE OF

HEART-LESS HATE-FUL HOR- RI- BLE HE- CU-BA ____

RI- BLE HE- CU- BA ____

MM ♩=160

— REPRISE —

HE- CU- BA __ IS A MEAN OLD WITCH __ WITH A HEART OF STONE __ AND A

BAG OF TRICKS_ TO TRICK YA ____

SHE'LL PRE-TEND_ TO BE NICE AS PIE _ BUT IF YOU LOOK_ IN HER

E-VIL EYE_ SHE'LL FIX YA ____ SO

HUN-TERS_ TAKE CARE BE- WARE OF

HEART-LESS HATE-FUL HOR- RI- BLE HE-CU-BA _____

IF I HAD A HORSESHOE (MATHEW)

IF I HAD A HORSE - SHOE   I WOULD TRADE IT FOR A

WALK-ING STICK ___   AND WHEN _ MAR-Y LOU _ CAME ROUND _ I'D

STRUT A-ROUND WITH IT AND SHE'D SAY OH WHAT A
SPLEN-DID FEL-LA SO POS-I-TIVE-LY NEAT
HE'S SUCH A WELL DRESSED FEL-LA HIM I'D LIKE TO MEET

They Were Warned

The hon-ey will taste sweet but I put a po-tion in it that will

Knock him cold in a min-ute and while he's ly-ing there with his

Feet stuck in the air I'll re-lieve him of all his val-ua-bles

It's not my fault it's his own fault

AF-TER ALL HE WAS WARNED HE WAS WARNED

IT'S NOT MY FAULT IT'S HIS OWN FAULT

(CON VOCE)

HE WAS WARNED HE WAS WARNED HE WAS WARNED_____

IF I HAD A HORSESHOE (EPHRAM)

IF I HAD A HORSE-SHOE ___ I WOULD TRADE IT FOR A

FA-MOUS BOOK ___ AND WHEN ___ MAR-Y LOU ___ CAME ROUND ___ I'D

LET HER HAVE A LOOK ___ AND SHE'D SAY ___ " MY WHAT A

WELL-READ FEL-LA   SO LEARN-ED   AND SO SMART___

HE'S SUCH A   BRIL-LIANT FEL-LA   HE CAN HAVE MY HEART___

RUBATO *THEY WERE WARNED* REPRISE

HIS   EYES ARE GO-ING TO ROLL TO THE BACK OF HIS HARD HEAD AS HE

FALLS TO THE GROUND AS IF DEAD   AND WHILE HE'S IN A TRANCE

I WILL HAVE A CHANCE TO RE- LIEVE HIM OF ALL — HIS POS- SES- SIONS

Tempo   mm ♩=144

IT'S NOT   MY   FAULT   IT'S THEIR   OWN   FAULT

AF- TER   ALL THEY WERE WARNED THEY WERE WARNED

IT'S NOT MY FAULT IT'S THEIR OWN FAULT

(CON VOCE)

THEY WERE WARNED THEY WERE WARNED THEY WERE WARNED

IF I HAD A HORSESHOE (CROESUS)

IF I HAD A HORSE- SHOE
I'D SWAP IT FOR A HE-LE
UM BAL-LOON
AND WHEN MAR-Y LOU CAME ROUND I'D
FLY HER TO THE MOON AND SHE'D SAY
OH WHAT A
DAR- FEL-LA
SUCH GEN-E-ROS-I-TY

He's such a kind - ly fel - la He's the one for me___

AHA

MOD ♩ = 132

Some-thing's smell-ing might-y fun-ny ___ Why does she in-

SIST ON GIV - ING ME HON - EY? A-
HA! O - HO SHE THINKS I DON'T
KNOW SHE'S THAT WITCH WHICH I WAS WARNED A - BOUT THAT
WITCH FOR WHICH I'D BET - TER WATCH OUT A-

HA I SEE SHE'S OUT – TO GET
ME WELL SHE'D BET- TER THINK AND THINK A-GAIN – IF SHE
THINKS I'LL LET HER DO ME IN
SHE'LL
TRY TO WIN OUR CON - FI - DENCE THEN FLEECE US

WELL SHE'LL SOON SEE SHE'S NOT AS SMART AS

CROE-SUS IS! A-

HA O HO! YOU THINK I DON'T

KNOW YOU'RE THAT WITCH WHICH I WAS WARNED A-BOUT THAT

WITCH FOR WHICH I'D BET-TER WATCH OUT!

SO HIGH SO WIDE SO DEEP

Gospel 4 ♩=132

SO ___ LONG ___ SO ___ WIDE

So ___ DEEP   YOU CAN'T GET A-ROUND IT YOU CAN'T SWIM O-VER IT YOU

CAN'T WADE A-CROSS IT   NO NO NO ___   YOU CAN'T GET A-ROUND IT YOU

CAN'T SWIM O-VER IT YOU CAN'T WADE A-CROSS IT   NO NO NO ___

So ___ LONG   So ___ THICK

So _____ TALL You Can't Get A-Round it You Can't Go Through_ it You

Can't Get O - ver It No No No__ You Can't Get A-Round it You

Can't Go Through_ it You Can't Get O - ver It No No No__

So _____ wide So _____ Rough

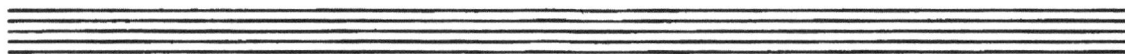

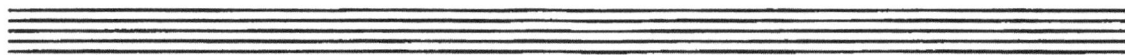

So Long - So Wide, Dance

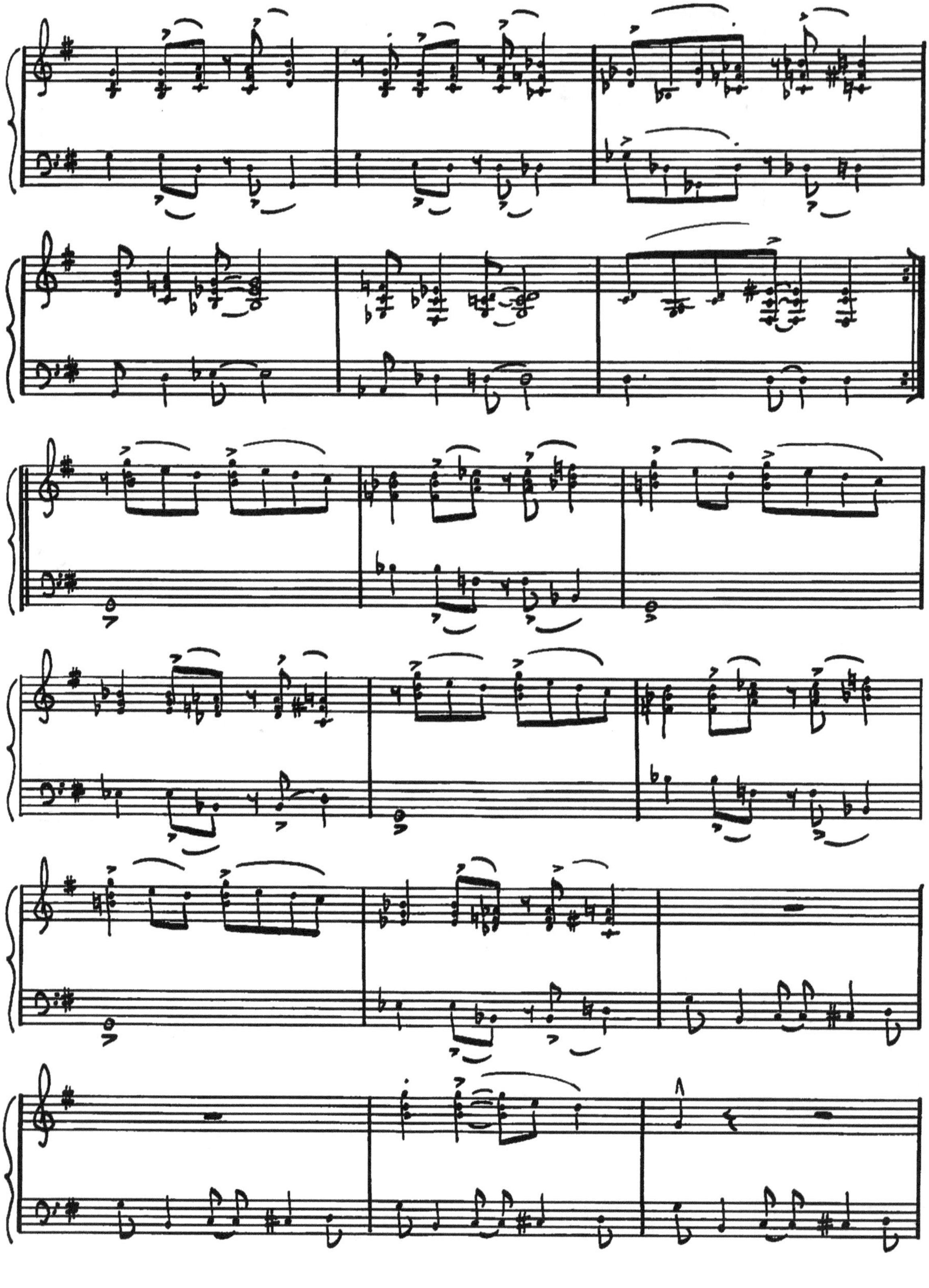

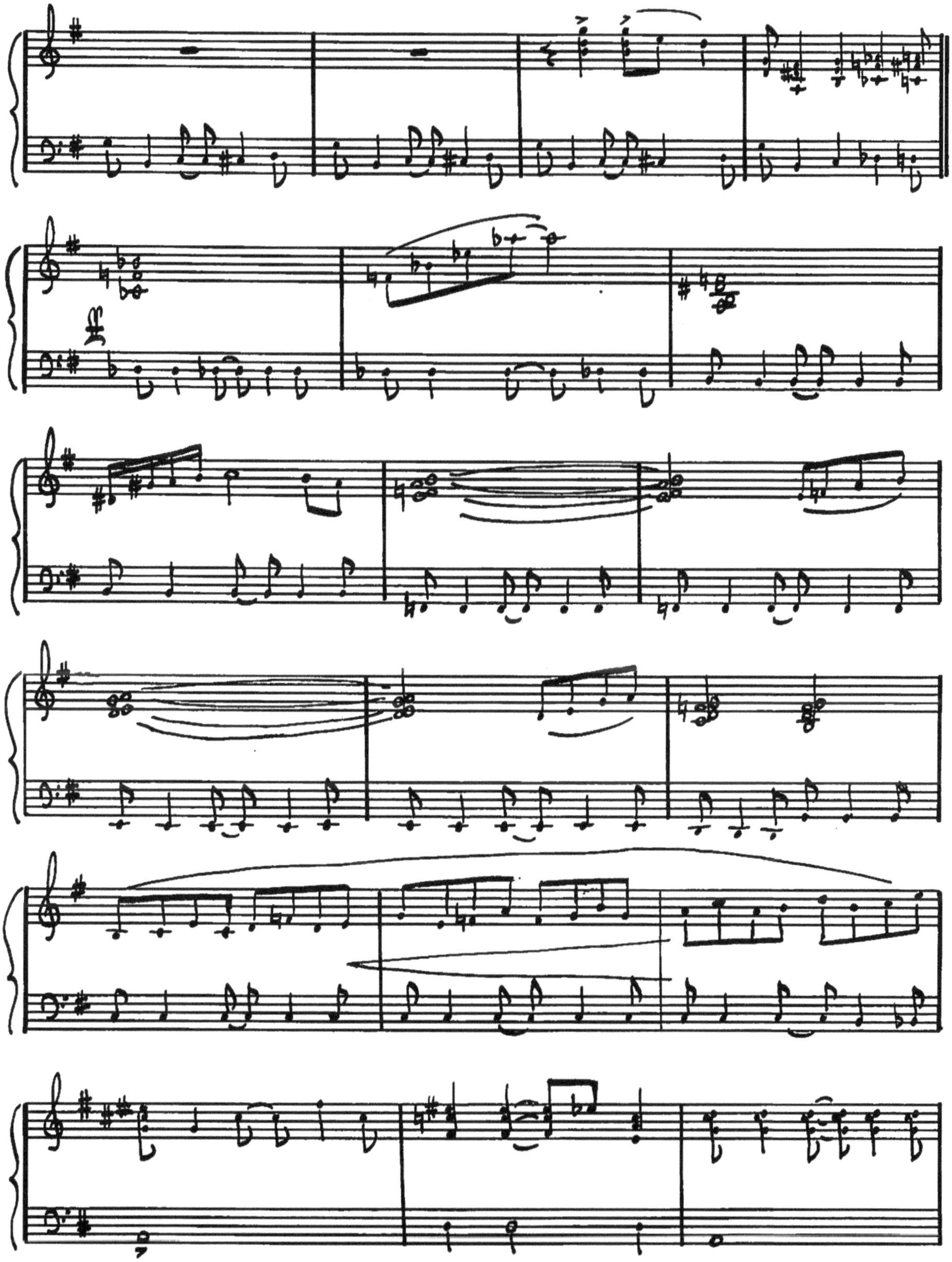

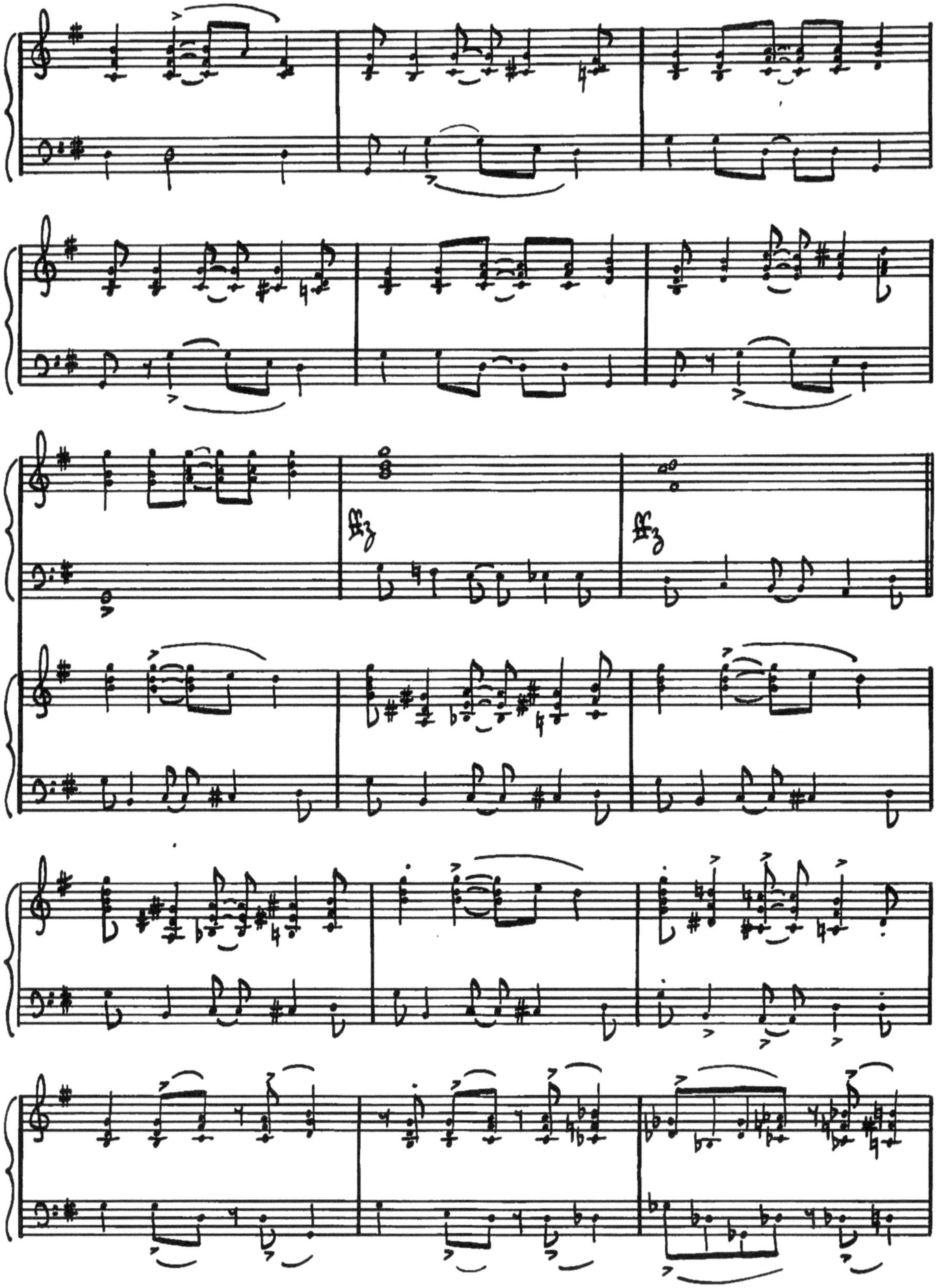
ffz
ffz

Segue

Slower MM = ♩ = 96

So___ Long   So___ Wide

So___ Deep   You Can't Get A-Round it You Can't Swim O-ver it You

CAN'T WADE A-CROSS IT NO NO NO___ YOU CAN'T GET A-ROUND IT YOU

CAN'T SWIM O-VER IT YOU CAN'T WADE A-CROSS IT NO NO NO___

SO___ LONG SO___ THICK

SO___ TALL YOU CAN'T GET A-ROUND IT YOU CAN'T GO THROUGH___ IT YOU

CAN'T GET O-VER IT NO NO NO — YOU CAN'T GET A-ROUND IT YOU
CAN'T GO THROUGH — IT YOU CAN'T GET O-VER IT NO NO NO —
RUBATO
SO HIGH —

So High, Exit Music

mm ♩=92

So Long You Can't get a-Round it So wide You Can't swim o-ver it So Deep You Can't wade a-cross it So Long You Can't get a-Round it So Thick You Can't go ___ through it So Tall You Can't get o-ver it

So wide you can't get a-round it   So rough you

Can't climb up it   So steep you can't get o-ver it

(On Cue.)

THEY WERE WARNED (Reprise)

THEY ARE MIGHT-Y HAND-SOME WOLVES BUT IF THEY ON-LY KNEW WHAT THIS

CLEV-ER LIT-TLE FOX IS GOIN' TO DO AF-TER SUP-ER WHEN THEY REST I'LL BE

FEATH-ER-ING MY NEST AS I DI- VEST THEM OF THEIR LIVES AND THEIR BE-LONG-INGS

TEMPO ♩ = 116

TOM TOM

IT'S NOT

MY FAULT___ IT'S THEIR OWN FAULT___ AF-TER

ALL THEY WERE WARNED___ THEY WERE WARNED _____ IT'S NOT

MY FAULT___ IT'S THEIR OWN FAULT___ THEY WERE

RUBATO

WARNED THEY WERE WARNED THEY WERE WARNED

V.S.

IF I HAD A HORSE SHOE — REPRISE

IF I HAD A HORSE-SHOE

I WOULD TRADE IT FOR A

WALK-ING STICK — AND WHEN MAR-Y LOU — CAME ROUND I'D

STRUT A-ROUND WITH IT — AND SHE'D SAY OH WHAT A

SPLEN-DID FEL-LA SO POS-I- TIVE-LY NEAT —

HE'S SUCH A WELL DRESSED FEL-LA HIM I'D LIKE TO MEET —

IF I HAD A HORSE-SHOE

I WOULD TRADE IT FOR A FA-MOUS BOOK __ AND WHEN __ MAR-Y LOU __

__ CAME ROUND __ I'D LET __ HER HAVE __ A LOOK __ SHE'D SAY

MY WHAT A WELL-READ FELT LA So LEARN -ED

AND SO SMART
HE'S SUCH A BRIL-LIANT FEL-LA
HE CAN HAVE MY HEART
IF I HAD A HORSE
SHOE
I'D SWAP IT FOR A HE-LI UM BAL-LOON
AND WHEN MAR-Y LOU CAME ROUND I'D
FLY HER TO THE MOON

SHE'D SAY OH WHAT A
FEL-LA
SUCH GEN-ER-OS-I-TY
HE'S SUCH A
KIND-LY FEL-LA
HE'S THE ONE FOR ME
IF I HAD A THUMB-TACK
I WOULD TRADE IT FOR SOME

EL-mer's Glue _ AND WHEN MAR-Y LOU _ CAME ROUND _ SHE'D

STICK TO YOU KNOW WHO _ AND I'D SAY OH WHAT A

LUCK-Y FEL-LA FOR-TU-NATE AS CAN BE _

I'M SUCH A HAP-PY FEL-LA MAR-Y LOU IS STUCK ON ME _

OH WHAT A LUCK-Y FEL-LA

FOR-TU-NATE AS CAN BE___ I'M SUCH A

HAP-PY FEL-LA MAR-Y LOU IS STUCK ON ME___ MAR-Y

REPEAT FOR FADE

LOU IS STUCK ON ME___ MAR-Y

You Can Do What You Wanna Do - Reprise

The

Tree of life has fruit ripe for the pick- ing ____

If you want a share you've got to be firm ___

____ Catch-ing an ex- tra

FOR- TY WINKS_ IS EAS- Y___ BUT THE
EAR- LY BIRD IS OUT THERE CATCH-ING THE WORM
YOU CAN GET WHAT YOU WAN-NA GET YOU CAN
GO WHERE YOU WAN-NA GO YOU CAN DO WHAT YOU WAN-NA DO

Lyrics visible under the staves:
BY DO-ING IT   YOU CAN
BY DO-ING IT   BY
BO-ING IT   BY DO-ING IT

AHA Reprise

♩ = 144

Things are look-ing kind-a shad-y ___ Some-thing is fa-

mil-iar a-bout that lad-y ___ A-

ha oh wow! I'm on ___ to her

now she's that same old witch we met be-fore ___ and she's

UP TO HER SAME OLD TRICKS ONCE MORE _____ A-

HA! OH YES UN-LESS I MISS MY

GUESS SHE WILL TRY TO KILL US IN OUR BEDS _ BY THE

CAPS WE'RE WEAR-ING ON OUR HEADS _____ SHE

THINKS WE'RE FOOLED BY THE NICE WAY THAT SHE TREATS US
BUT I'LL SHOW HER SHE CAN'T THINK AS FAST AS
CROE - SUS CAN! A HA! OH
WOW WE'RE ON _ TO HER NOW SHE'S THAT

SAME OLD WITCH WE MET BE-FORE _ AND SHE'S UP TO HER SAME OLD
TRICKS ONCE MORE _ A- HA! OH
YES! UN-LESS WE MISS MY GUESS SHE WILL
TRY TO KILLS US IN OUR BEDS _ BY THE CAPS WE'RE WEAR-ING

ON OUR HEADS SHE THINKS WE'RE FOOLED BY THE
NICE WAY THAT SHE TREATS US BUT WE'LL
SHOW HER SHE CAN'T THINK AS FAST AS CROE-US US
CAN

Throwing Stones

Bluesy ♩ = 92

WHEN YOU'RE OUT TO DO AN-OTH-ER IN ____

LOOK OUT YOU DON'T BURST YOUR BAL- LOON WITH YOUR OWN PIN ____

____ WHILE YOU'RE TRY-ING TO

BLOCK MY PATH___ SOME-ONE ELSE MAY GET___ THE LAST LAUGH ON

YOU BE- CARE-FUL WHEN YOU

STEP ON TOES___ OR YOU MAY TRIP YOUR-SELF___

YOU COULD GET HIT IN THE BACK___ WHILE THROW-ING STONES___ AT

Some-one else ___ while you're bus-y dig-ging oth-er graves ___

Look out or the dirt might

Fly back in your face ___ you may

Dou-ble cross ___ with un- con-cern ___ but the e- vil that you

DO WILL TURN ON YOU ____

Accel ___ ___

MM = ♩ = 126

CALL-ING NAMES AND HURT-ING FOLKS ___ I CAN LIVE WITH-OUT ___

____ IT BE- FORE YOU TRY TO CUT MY THROAT ___

THINK A- BOUT ___ IT WHILE YOU'RE BUS-Y DIG-GING OTH-ER GRAVES ___

LOOK OUT OR THE DIRT MIGHT

FLY BACK IN YOUR FACE ___ YOU MAY

DOU-BLE CROSS___ WITH UN- CON-CERN ___ BUT THE E-VIL THAT YOU

DO WILL TURN ON YOU _____

FINALE

mm ♩=160

No use sit-ting wait-ing for some-thing to hap - pen ____

Sit-ting twid-dling your fin-gers and your toes ____

You can be out

MAK-ING YOUR OWN THING HAP-PEN
IN-STEAD OF SIT-TING AT HOME SCRATCH-ING YOUR NOSE
YOU CAN GET WHAT YOU WAN-NA GET YOU CAN
GO WHERE YOU WAN-NA GO YOU CAN DO WHAT YOU WAN-NA DO

BY - DO-ING IT
TO-DAY WILL BE YES-TER-DAY TO- MOR-ROW
IF YOU WANT TO SIT A-ROUND AND WAIT
YOU WILL JUST BE

HUN - GRI - ER — TO - MOR - ROW _____ AND

YOU WON'T HAVE AN-Y GRITS TO PUT ON YOUR PLATE _____

_ YOU CAN GET WHAT YOU WAN-NA GET _ YOU CAN

GO WHERE YOU WAN-NA GO _ YOU CAN DO WHAT YOU WAN-NA DO_

BY_ DO-ING IT.

Good Old Irma

COUNTRY FEEL

MM = ♩ – 96

Good old

Ir - ma   Good old   Ir - ma   You'd

Think she was the   Soul of dain - ti - ness   But she

Nev - er cleans the   House then blames the   Chil-dren for the   mess that's good old

IR- MA SHE LIKES TO LIE A- ROUND ALL DAY
AND GRUM- BLE AND GROAN BUT WHEN SHE'S NOT DO- ING
THAT SHE'S ON THE TE- LE- PHONE WITH GOOD OLD FLO- RENCE
GOOD OLD FLO- RENCE SHE'S IR- MA'S BO- SOM

FRIEND AND THAT'S NOT ODD CAUSE THE TWO ARE SO A-
LIKE THEY'RE JUST LIKE TWO PEAS IN A POD FLO AND IR- MA
GOOD OLD IR- MA
HAND- ING OUT OR- DERS LIKE A QUEEN

GOOD   OLD   ROY- AL

HIGH- NESS   HOW CAN YOU   ACT SO DOG-GONE   MEAN

(DIALOG.)
ALL THOSE TWO EVER DO IS DRINK COFFEE, TALK ON THE PHONE
AND GO TO LUNCHES. OLD WOLFGANG IS OUT SLAVING AWAY
ALL DAY AND WHAT DOES HE COME HOME TO!

TO GOOD OLD IR- MA   GOOD OLD   IR- MA

WHO GREETS HIM AT THE DOOR WITH HER COM- PLAINTS
TO HEAR HER TALK YOU'D THINK THAT LIT-TLE KIDS SHOULD ALL BE
SAINTS THAT'S GOOD OLD IR- MA AS FOR THE KIDS HAN-SEL AND
GRE- TEL ______ YOU CAN BE SURE (THAT) THEY GET THE

CHORES WHILE IR-MA GETS A MAN-i-CURE GOOD OLD

IR-MA HAND-ING OUT OR-DERS LIKE A

QUEEN GOOD OLD ROY-AL

HIGH-NESS HOW COME YOU ACT SO DOG-GONE MEAN?

How Come You ACT So DoG - GonE

MeaN?

CHILDREN NEED DISCIPLINE

MOD. BLUESY

MM ♩=100

IT'S TIME FOR YOU TO TAKE CON-TROL FOR-GET A-BOUT DOC-TOR SPOCK
YOU LET 'EM HAVE THEIR WAY AND THAT'S WHY TO-DAY
WE GOT THE WORST KIDS ON THE BLOCK!

CHILD-REN NEED DIS-CI-PLINE__ LIKE A WILD HORSE NEEDS A ROPE__

IN-STEAD OF HO HO HO-ING LIKE SAN-TA CLAUSE__ YOU GOT-TA

LET 'EM KNOW__ WHO'S BOSS__

IT'S TIME YOU LAID IT ON THE LINE__ AND PUT YOU BIG FOOT DOWN HARD__

I WAS A KID ONCE TOO_ I KNOW WHAT KID'S WILL DO_ YOU
GIVE 'EM A FOOT THEY'LL TAKE A YARD
CHILD-REN NEED DIS-CI-PLINE_ LIKE A WILD HORSE NEEDS A ROPE_
IN-STEAD OF HO HO HO-ING LIKE SAN-TA CLAUSE_ YOU GOT-TA

LET 'em KNOW— WHO's BOSS ——— You

GOT-TA KEEP 'em HOP-PIN' AND KEEP 'em MOP-PIN' IF YOU

WAN-NA KEEP 'em IN THEIR PLA- CES YOU GOT-TA BE

ON YOUR GUARD— AND DIS-RE-GARD— THOSE SWEET AN-GEL FA-

CES
CHILD-REN NEED
DIS-CI-PLINE_ LIKE A
WILD HORSE NEEDS A ROPE ___
IN-STEAD OF
HO HO HO-ING LIKE
SAN-TA CLAUS_ YOU GOT-TA
LET 'EM KNOW_ WHO'S BOSS ___

Friendship

IN 2   mm ♩=144

Lyrics (melody line):

A FRIEND is there in a PINCH A FRIEND nev-er runs from trou-ble A FRIEND when you're in a fix I say A

Section markings: CHORUS, SOLO

SOLO   CHORUS

FRIEND   IS   THERE—   ON THE   DOU-BLE   A

SOLO   CHORUS

FRIEND   WILL NOT LET YOU   DOWN   A

SOLO   CHORUS

FRIEND   WHEN YOU'RE IN A   PIC- KLE   A

SOLO   CHORUS

FRIEND   IF HE'S GOT A   DIME—   A

SOLO
FRIEND
YOU'VE GOT A NIC - KLE
CHORUS
FRIEND - SHIP
FRIEND - SHIP
THERE'S NO BET- TER SHIP THAN

FRIEND-SHIP
A
SOLO
CHORUS
FRIEND IS THERE WHEN IT RAINS A
SOLO
CHORUS
FRIEND NOT JUST WHEN IT'S SUN-NY A
SOLO
CHO.
FRIEND WILL LAUGH AT ALL YOUR JOKES A

FRIEND ev-en THOUGH THEY'RE NOT FUN-NY A

FRIEND IS THERE WHEN YOU LOSE A

FRIEND NOT JUST WHEN YOU'RE WIN-NING A

FRIEND WHEN YOU'RE ALL TIED UP A

Solo

FRIEND　　　　　WILL GO AN EX-TRA IN-NING

Chorus

FRIEND-　　SHIP ___

FRIEND-　　SHIP ___

THERE'S NO BET-TER SHIP　　　THAN

FRIEND-SHIP
THERE ARE
TALL SHIPS
AND
SMALL SHIPS
AND
SCHOL-AR-SHIPS
AND
FEL-LOW-SHIPS
AND
EV-'RY
OTH-ER
KIND OF SHIP
BUT

FRIEND- SHIP ____

FRIEND- SHIP ____

THERE'S NO BET-TER SHIP THAN

FRIEND-SHIP

FRIEND - SHIP____

FRIEND - SHIP____

THERE'S NO BET-TER SHIP THAN

FRIEND-SHIP FRIEND-SHIP

Tree's Lament

Mm ♩=108

The rain comes

Down and it drops on me a bird sits down on my

branch then plops on me I ask you is that an-y way to treat a

tree then old Jack Frost puts the

FREEZE ON ME A DOG STOPS BY LIFTS HIS LEG AND WEE WEES ON ME I

ASK YOU IS THAT AN-Y WAY TO TREAT A TREE?

JUST LOOK AT ME I'M GOR-GEOUS THE

FIN-EST OF NA-TURE'S GREEN-ER-Y DECKED OUT ___ FROM

LIMB TO LEAF___ I'M A CRE-DIT TO THE SCEN-ER-Y THEN HERE YOU

COME MAK-ING MY HEAD ACHE AND YOU'VE GOT NO AS-PIR-

IN FOR ME TO TAKE I ASK YOU is THAT AN-Y WAY TO TREAT A

GOR-GEOUS TREE LIKE me IS THAT AN-Y

WAY TO TREAT A   TREE? _____

KID-KE-BOB

MOD. 4
Mm ♩=104

YOUNG AND SUC-CU-LENT SWEET AND TEN-DER BET-TER THAN FROGS OR FISH___

BROILED BOILED OR BAR-BE-QUED___ YOUNG-UNS

ARE MY FAV-O-RITE DISH___ THERE AIN'T NOTH-ING LIKE

FRENCH FRIED FIN-GERS   OR   A   FRENCH FRIED PIG   NOSE   AND

DO___ WEE I SURE DO LOVE___SNACK-ING   ON PLUMP PICK-LED TOES___

STUFFED YOUNG CHEEKS MAKE REAL GOOD EATS___

THEY'RE HARD TO RE-   SIST   BUT   WHEN IT COMES___ TO

GOUR-MET TREATS_ KID-KE-BOB TOPS THE LIST__
KID-KE-BOB KID-KE-BOB BOB_ CAN CHASE A-WAY MY GLOOM_
KID-KE-BOB I LOVE IT AL-MOST AS MUCH AS
RID-ING ON MY BROOM____ KID-KE-BOB

KiD - Ke - BoB BoB___   KiD Ke BoB   KiD - Ke - BoB BoB

NO WAY

Mod. mm ♩ = 116

NO WAY___

WOULD I EV- ER SEND MY AN- GELS OFF TO STAY WITH STRANG-

ERS AL- THOUGH LAST SEP- TEM- BER I GAVE IN AND LET THEM

GO WITH THE JUN- IOR RANG- ERS THAT WAS JUST FOR O- VER

NIGHT NOTH-ING MORE THAN O-VER NIGHT
NO SIR THERE'S NO WAY THAT I'LL BE GIV-ING IN-TO
HER NOT THIS TIME BE-FORE SHE COULD
TWIST ME ROUND HER FIN-GER BUT NO MORE YOU CAN BET IN THIS. I'M

BURN-ing UP AND HOP-PING MAD   THEY'RE MY KIDS AND I'M THEIR

DAD   AND   I WANT TO KNOW THERE'S A   ROOF O-VER-HEAD AND THEIR

STO-MACHS ARE FED WHEN THEY'RE TUCKED IN-TO BED _____   FOR WHER-

EV-ER I AM _____   RICH OR POOR AS I AM _____

FOR MY HAN- SEL AND GRE - TEL IT'S

Home _____

The Twilight Zone

MM ♩=108

TURN YOUR EYES___ IN-SIDE OUT___ AND SEARCH THE BACK OF YOUR

MIND THERE IN A CORN-ER IN A SOFT GREY LIGHT YOU'LL

FIND WHAT'S KNOWN AS THE TWI- LIGHT ZONE___

IT'S A PLACE WHERE NOTH-ING'S... BLACK OR WHITE IT'S

AL-WAYS MAY-BE OR MIGHT AND YOU'RE AL-WAYS JUST ON THE

VERGE OF THINGS... THAT ARE AL-MOST BUT NOT QUITE AND THOUGH

THINGS THAT YOU SEE AP-PEAR TO BE REAL THEY'RE NEV-ER AS REAL AS THEY

Seem it's a little like being half asleep. You're

almost but not quite in a dream. So

turn your eyes outside in and search the back of your

mind there in a corner in a soft grey light you'll

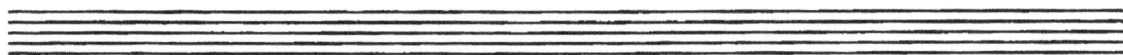

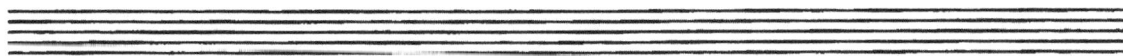

TWILIGHT ZONE - DANCE

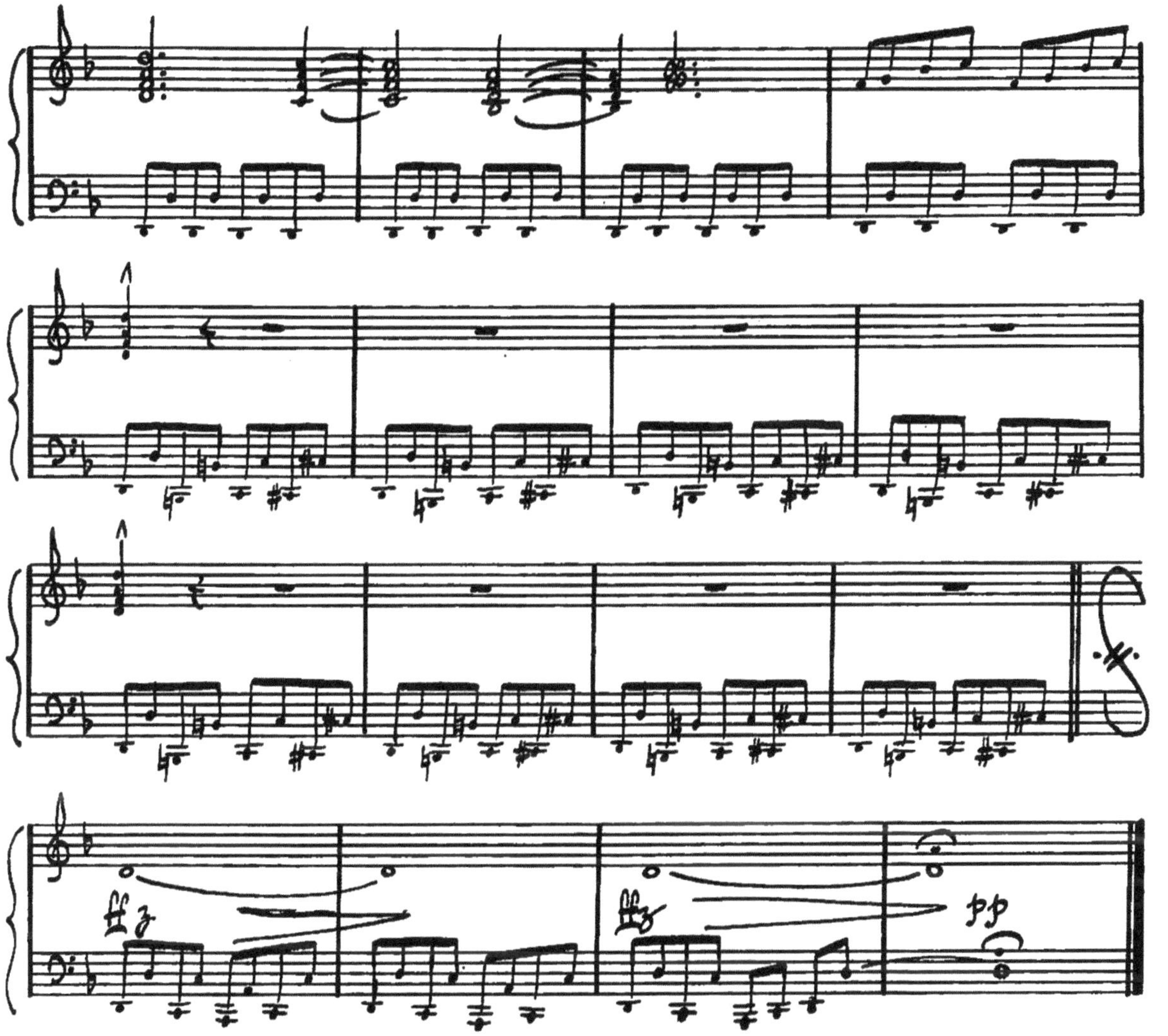
ffz
ffz
pp

www.ingramcontent.com/pod-product-compliance
Lightning Source LLC
Chambersburg PA
CBHW080505110426

42742CB00017B/3002